For my precious husband, Jerry,
with loving thanks for all you do!
Especially for driving 6000 miles so I could experience the Oregon Trail.
You are a special gift from God, and I am so thankful for you!
I love you with all my heart.
Janna

Song of Solomon 5:16—
"This is my beloved and this is my friend."

CONTENTS

SEARCHING FOR TRUTH—
A BIBLE STUDY YOU CAN DO!

Hey! Guess what? Molly, Sam (the great detective beagle), and I are heading out West to follow the Oregon Trail. Doesn't that sound exciting? By the way, my name is Max, and we want you to join us in an exciting adventure in God's Word as we travel across the hot, dusty wilderness and discover one of God's brave explorers—a man named Abram.

Did you know that the pioneers who followed the Oregon Trail left behind their homes, country, and families to begin a new life in a land that they had never seen in the hope of having a better life? WHAT about Abram? WHO is this brave explorer? WHY did he leave his home and journey to a land he didn't know? WHY did God change his name from Abram to Abraham? And WHAT did he do to have a life full of blessings and to be called God's friend? Isn't that awesome to think that God would call you His friend?

You have so much to discover about Abraham as you study God's map, the Bible—the source of all truth—and ask God's Spirit to lead and guide you. You also have this book, which is an inductive Bible study.

That word *inductive* means you go straight to the Bible *yourself* to investigate the life of Abraham in the Book of Genesis and discover what it means, instead of depending on what someone else says it means.

So pack up your gear, and don't forget God's map! Let's begin our westward trek over rugged terrain to discover what it means to walk by faith and become God's friend. Westward ho! Let's go!

I'm ready to go!

THINGS YOU'LL NEED
▼

NEW AMERICAN STANDARD BIBLE
(UPDATED EDITION)—OR, PREFERABLY, THE
NEW INDUCTIVE STUDY BIBLE (NISB)

PEN OR PENCIL

COLORED PENCILS

INDEX CARDS

A DICTIONARY

THIS WORKBOOK

1

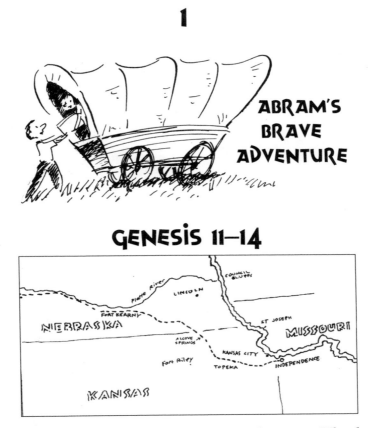

ABRAM'S BRAVE ADVENTURE

GENESIS 11–14

"All right! The SUV is packed and ready to go. Uh-oh, where's Sam? Sam, where are you? Come on, boy, we're ready to go. Watch out—here he comes! Quick! Move out of the way! Whew—just in time. Sam, settle down, boy. You almost ran over Molly.

"Okay, let's pile in the SUV and hit the road. Our first stop is St. Louis, Missouri, where many of the pioneers arrived from their homes to get ready for the adventure of their life. So pull out God's map—the Bible—and as we head west for our big adventure, let's find out about God's brave explorer. WHO is Abram and WHY did he leave his home? Was it for the spirit of adventure or a better life, like it was for some of our pioneers? Let's open God's map to find out."

FOLLOWING GOD'S BRAVE EXPLORER

We are on our way. As you open God's map to discover WHO Abram is, WHAT is the first thing you need to do? Do you know? You've got it! Pray. Bible study should always begin with prayer.

We need God to be our Wagon Master as we begin our journey on the Oregon Trail. The wagon master was in charge of the entire wagon train. He made all the decisions about whether to go on or stop. He also decided which trail they should take. His word was law!

Just like the wagon master took care of the pioneers on their journey, we need God to direct us and teach us by His Spirit as we begin our journey in His Word, so that we can understand what He says and make sure we handle His Word accurately. Let's pray, and then we can start reading God's map.

Heavenly Father, we praise You for being our Shepherd who leads us as we study Your Word. Open our eyes so that we can see truth as we study Abram's life. Open our hearts so that we can understand what Your Word means. Help us to apply all that we learn to our lives so that we can be more like Jesus. We want to please You. We love You and ask these things in Jesus' name. Amen.

Abram's life begins in the Book of Genesis, which is known as the book of beginnings. So as we start our research on our brave explorer, we need to put ourselves in context by reviewing the Book of Genesis.

WHAT is context? Context is the setting in which something is found. This is very important in Bible study. Context is a combination of two words: *con,* which means "with," and *text,* which means "what is written." So when you look for context in the Bible, you look at the verses and chapters surrounding the passage you are studying, such as looking at the whole Book of Genesis, as well as seeing how the passage fits into the whole Bible.

Context also includes:

✝ The place something happens. (This is geographical context, such as knowing where Abram lived. Did he live in the land of Canaan or in the United States?)

✝ The time in history an event happens. (This is historical context, such as, did Abram live before Noah and the flood or after the flood?)

✝ The customs of a group of people. (This is cultural context. For instance, did Abram live in a tent or in a house like we do today?)

If you have already studied Genesis Part One, *God's Amazing Creation,* and Genesis Part Two, *Digging Up the Past,* then you have discovered for yourself that Genesis is a book of generations. A generation is what is brought into being. It shows where something or someone came from. A generation shows the order of birth, the family history.

In Genesis 2:4 we see the generations of the heavens and the earth. In Genesis 5:1 we see the generations of Adam. We see Noah's generations in Genesis 6:9; Shem, Ham, and Japheth's generations in Genesis 10:1; and Shem's generations in Genesis 11:10. WHERE does Abram fit into these generations? Let's find out.

Turn to your Observation Worksheets on page 157. Observation Worksheets are pages that have the Bible text printed out for you to use as you do your research on the life of Abram.

Now read Genesis 11:24-32 and mark every reference to Abram in a special way by coloring *Abram* blue, along with

any pronouns that also refer to Abram. WHAT are pronouns?
Check out Max and Molly's map below.

PRONOUNS

Pronouns are words that take the place of nouns. A
noun is a person, place, or thing. A pronoun stands in for
a noun! Here's an example: "Molly and Max are heading
west to travel the Oregon Trail. They will have to drive
about 3000 miles from their home to get to the end of
the trail." The word *they* is a pronoun because it takes the
place of Molly's and Max's names in the second sentence.
It is another word we use to refer to Molly and Max.
Watch for these other pronouns when you are marking
people:

I	you	he	she
me	yours	him	her
mine		his	hers

we	it
our	its
they	them

Now that you have marked *Abram,* go back and mark one
of the key phrases in the Book of Genesis, *"these are the generations of,"* by putting a blue box around this key phrase.

Great! Now let's ask some questions. An explorer always
gets the facts by asking lots of questions before he or she
begins a journey.

Let's see WHAT we can learn about Abram and his family
by asking the 5 W's and an H questions. What are the 5 W's
and an H? They are the WHO, WHAT, WHERE, WHEN,
WHY, and HOW questions.

1. Asking WHO helps you find out:

WHO wrote this?

WHOM are we reading about?

To WHOM was it written?

WHO said this or did that?

2. WHAT helps you understand:

WHAT is the author talking about?

WHAT are the main things that happen?

3. WHERE helps you learn:

WHERE did something happen?

WHERE did they go?

WHERE was this said?

When we discover a WHERE, we double-underline the <u>WHERE</u> in green.

4. WHEN tells us about time. We mark it with a green clock like this: 🕐

WHEN tells us:

WHEN did this event happen or WHEN will it happen?

WHEN did the main characters do something? It helps us to follow the order of events.

5. WHY asks questions like:

WHY did he say that?

WHY did they go there?

WHY did this happen?

6. HOW lets you figure out things like:

HOW is something to be done?

HOW did people know something had happened?

Now get the facts.

WHOSE generations are these in Genesis 11:27?

_____

Looking back at Genesis 11:10, we see that Terah came from the generations of Shem. Let's find out WHO is in Terah's family tree.

Genesis 11:27 WHO did Terah become the father of?

_____

Genesis 11:27 WHO did Haran become the father of?

_____

Genesis 11:29 WHO was Abram's wife?

_____

Genesis 11:30 WHAT do we see about Sarai?

_____

Genesis 11:31 WHERE did Terah's family live?

_____

Genesis 11:31 WHERE did Terah settle his family?

_____

Genesis 11:32 WHAT happened to Terah in Haran?

_____

Now go back and read Genesis 11:27-29 again so you can fill in part of Terah's family tree below. We'll complete his family tree as we continue our journey in God's Word.

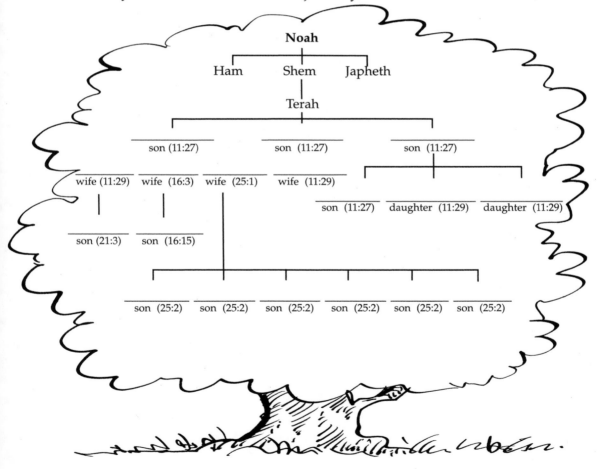

Wow! Look at all you have discovered from just a small portion of God's map! You are going to make quite an explorer!

Before we arrive in St. Louis, there is one more thing you need to do. A brave explorer for God needs to be prepared for the journey that God has planned for him or her, and the only way to be ready for whatever God has for you is to know His Word. Hiding God's Word in your heart will keep you on the right road when the going gets tough and will give you hope as you put your faith in God.

As part of your journey across the wilderness, you need to learn a memory verse each week so that by the time you arrive in Oregon City, Oregon, you will be fully equipped for whatever God has planned for your life.

To discover this week's verse, use your navigational skills to find the correct path in the maze below. Then fill in the blanks with the correct words on the lines after the maze.

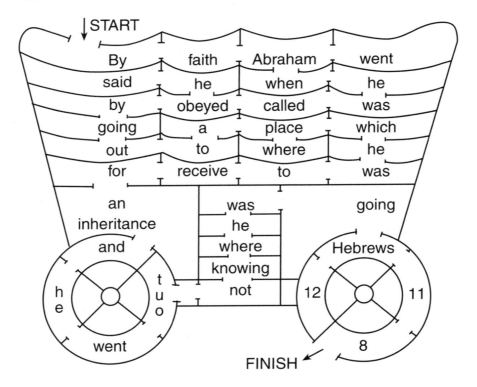

_____ _____ _____, _____ _____

_____ _____, _____ _____ _____

_____ _____ _____ _____ _____

_____ _____ _____ ____ ____

_____; _____ ____ _____ _____,

_____ _____ _____ ____ _____

_____.

—Hebrews ____ : ____

Way to go! Now practice saying it aloud three times in a row, three times every day!

GOD CALLS ABRAM

"Look!" exclaimed Molly as Max, Sam, and their families headed through the park in St. Louis toward the St. Louis arch. "There it is—straight ahead. I can't believe how big it is!"

"Oh, wow! Hurry up, everyone. I can't wait to see it up close. Do we really get to ride all the way to the top of the arch, Dad?"

"You sure do, Max," answered Luke, Max's dad. "We can ride all the way to the top in a tiny five-passenger capsule. Then we can get out inside the top of the arch and look through some tiny little windows."

"This is going to be so awesome," Max stated. "How high up will we be?"

Max's Aunt Kathy, who is Molly's mom, answered as she read from their guidebook. "The arch is one of the United States' greatest and tallest monuments. It is 630 feet tall!"

"Cool," replied Max. "We're almost there. Let's race, Molly."

"Okay," Molly laughed. "Go," she yelled as she took off across the grass to beat Max and be the first one to touch the arch.

Now as we head inside the arch with Max, Molly, Sam, and their families to take a ride to the top, let's talk with our Wagon Master—God. Then we can pull out God's map and discover what's happening with our brave explorer Abram.

As we ride to the top of the arch, turn to your Observation Worksheet on Genesis 11:24-32 on pages 158-159.

Let's review what we saw yesterday as we discovered WHO was Abram's family.

Genesis 11:31 WHERE did they live?

_____ of the_____

WHERE was Terah (Abram's father) headed to with Abram, Lot (Terah's grandson and Abram's nephew), and Sarai (Abram's wife)?

The _____ of _____

But as they began their journey they ended up WHERE?

In _____

Genesis 11:32 And then WHAT happened?

_____ died.

Now WHY did Terah decide to move his family? Do you know? Let's find out by doing some cross-referencing. WHAT is *cross-referencing?* Cross-referencing is where we compare Scripture with Scripture by going to other passages in the Bible. This is a very important Bible study tool that we can use as we search out the meaning of Scripture because we know that Scripture never contradicts Scripture.

Let's take out God's map (the Bible). Look up and read Acts 7:1-5.

Looking at Acts 7:2-3, WHY did Abraham (Abram) decide to leave his country?

_____

_____

Acts 7:2 WHEN did God speak to Abraham?

When he was in _____, before he

lived in _____

Acts 7:3 WHAT did God tell Abraham to do?

_____

_____

Acts 7:4 WHAT did Abraham do?

_____

Acts 7:4 WHAT did God have Abraham do after his father died?

_____

Look up and read Isaiah 51:1,2.

Isaiah 51:2 WHEN did God call Abraham?

_____

Isaiah 51:2 WHAT happened after God called Abraham?

God _____ him and _____ him.

Now let's look up one more verse—your memory verse.
Have you practiced it today? Look up and read Hebrews 11:8.

WHAT did Abraham do when he was called?

He o __ __ __ __ d.

HOW? By _____

_____

Did Abraham know where he was going?

_____

Take a look at the map on the next page to see the route that Abraham took to get to Canaan.

Now we know WHY Terah decided to move his family. Acts 7 tells us that God appeared to Abraham and told him to leave his country and relatives to go to a land He would show him. Isaiah 51 and Hebrews 11 show us that God called

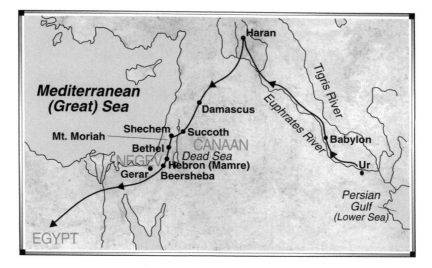

Abraham. In Hebrews we also see that Abraham obeyed, not knowing where he was going. Isn't that awesome?

Abraham had faith. He trusted and followed God when God called him, even though he didn't know where it would lead him.

HOW about you? Have you put your faith in God? Are you willing to follow Him? Do you obey when God shows you what you need to be doing? Think about how you respond to God's call.

We'll uncover more as we continue our journey tomorrow. Now that we've made it to the top of the arch, let's practice our memory verse as we take in the fantastic view of St. Louis from 630 feet above the ground!

LEARNING TO FOLLOW GOD

"Wasn't it awesome being in the top of the arch?" Max asked Molly as they were eating breakfast the next morning.

"Yeah, I loved it," replied Molly. "But getting up there was another thing. That little capsule was sooooo small and stuffy. I didn't think those four minutes would ever end."

Max laughed as he replied, "Sam didn't like it too much either. I have never heard him bark so much, have you?"

Max's mom, Jena, responded, "Sam, you almost got us kicked out of the arch. Now be a good dog today as we head to Independence, Missouri—one of the three 'jumping-off' places for the pioneers. It will be the official start of our journey on the Oregon Trail."

"Yeah!" Max and Molly exclaimed. "We're ready to go!"

How about you? Have you talked with your Wagon Master? Let's begin the next leg of our journey. Turn to page 159 to Genesis 12. Today as we read our map we need to mark some key words.

What are *key words?* Key words are words that pop up more than once. They are called key words because they help unlock the meaning of the chapter or book that you are studying and give you clues about what is most important in a passage of Scripture.

✚ Key words are usually used over and over again.

✚ Key words are important.

✚ Key words are used by the writer for a reason.

Once you discover a key word, you need to mark it in a special way using a special color or symbol so that you can immediately spot it in Scripture. Don't forget to mark any pronouns that go with the key words, too! So let's get started. Read Genesis 12 and mark the following key words:

Lord (draw a purple triangle and color it yellow)

Abram (color it blue)

bless (blessing, blessed) (put a blue cloud around it and color it pink)

land (double-underline it in green and color it blue)

altar (draw a red box around it)

Lot (color it orange)

famine (box it in black and color it brown)

Don't forget to mark anything that tells you WHERE by double-underlining the <u>WHERE</u> in green. And don't forget to mark anything that tells you WHEN by drawing a green clock like this: 🕐

Now let's make a list to see what God promised Abram.

Genesis 12:1 I will give you a l __ __ d that I will show you.

Genesis 12:2 I will make you a _____   _____.

Genesis 12:2 I will _____ you and make your

n ___ ___ ___ great.

Genesis 12:7 To your _____ I will give this

_____.

As we follow Abram on our journey of faith, we need to watch and see what God does. Does God keep His promises to Abram? Remember, Sarai is barren at this point. *Barren* means that she and Abram have never had a child, yet God has promised to make Abram a great nation and to give his descendants this land. In order for God to make Abram a great nation, we know that someday He will give Abram and Sarai a child.

Now let's continue to get the facts by asking the 5 W's and an H.

Genesis 12:4 HOW old is Abram when he departs from Haran?

_____

Can you believe that Abram is 75 years old, and he doesn't have any children yet? (By the way, did you remember to put a green clock over Abram's age?)

Genesis 12:5 WHOM did Abram take with him?

_____

Genesis 12:5 WHERE are they headed?

_____

Genesis 12:6 HOW far did Abram get?

_____

Take a look at your map. Check out where Abram stopped and circle the place in green.

Genesis 12:7 WHAT happened in this verse?

_____

_____

Genesis 12:7 WHAT did Abram build there?

_____

Genesis 12:8 WHAT did Abram do here?

_____

Genesis 12:9 WHERE did Abram journey?

_____

Genesis 12:10 WHAT happens?

_____

Genesis 12:11-13 WHAT did Abram tell Sarai to do when they got to Egypt?

_____

_____

Genesis 12:15 WHAT did Pharaoh do?

_____

Genesis 12:16 HOW was Abram treated?

_____

Genesis 12:17 WHAT did the Lord do?

_____

Genesis 12:17 WHY?

_____

Genesis 12:18 WHAT did Pharaoh do?

_____

_____

Look at all we uncovered on our journey today! As Abram begins his journey to follow God, he comes to Shechem where God appears to him and reminds him of His promise. HOW does Abram respond? He builds an altar and worships God.

Then as he continues his journey to Ai, not only do we see Abram build another altar to worship God, but we also see him call on the name of the Lord.

Did you know that in the Bible a person's name reveals his character? So for Abram to call on God's name, he was recognizing God for WHO He is—His character and His ways. To worship God is to acknowledge His worth, to give Him the honor and reverence that is due Him. It is praising God for WHO He is.

God had been faithful to lead Abram in his journey to the land He had promised, so Abram built the altars to worship God and call on His name.

But what happens next? There's a famine in the land and, instead of asking God what he should do, Abram heads off on his own. He heads down to Egypt. Did you know that Egypt is a picture of the world?

Not only do we see Abram taking his own route instead of God's as he heads to Egypt, but we also see that he gets himself into some trouble. Abram tells Sarai that he is afraid that Pharaoh will kill him if he finds out that she is his wife, so he tells her to tell Pharaoh that she is his sister. This shows us that Abram fears man more than he fears God.

Just look at the trouble that brings. God strikes Pharaoh and his household because Pharaoh has taken Sarai.

WHAT a mess! Is Abram perfect? No, we have just seen Abram make a very big mistake. But does God change His mind about His promise to Abram? No way! God rescues Abram by striking Pharaoh and his household.

Even though Abram failed, God didn't reject him. He still loves Abram and has a plan for his life. This shows us that God is a God of grace and mercy. Grace is unearned favor. We don't earn God's love and forgiveness—it is a gift. We also see that God is long-suffering. This means God is patient with us as we learn to rely and depend on Him. Abram is just beginning his journey of faith, learning to trust and depend on God.

HOW about you? WHAT is your relationship like with God? Abram was scared of Pharaoh. Have you ever been scared and said something you shouldn't have said in order to get out of a difficult situation that you were in? _____ Yes _____ No

If you have, write out what you did on the lines below.

_____

_____

Now pray and ask God to help you trust Him the next time you are afraid. Ask Him to give you the courage to do the right thing!

All right—you are on your way on your journey of faith! Don't forget to practice your memory verse three times in a row three times today!

CONFLICT AND CHOICES

As the SUV pulled into the National Frontier Trails Center in Independence, Max said, "Independence, Missouri—one of the three 'jumping-off' places for the pioneers. Did you know our guidebook says that just west of here is the place where the pioneers filled up their water barrels before heading west?"

"That's right, Max," said Max's Uncle Kyle, who is Molly's dad. "When the emigrants arrived here, the first thing they did was look for a wagon train they could join up with. Then they needed to get outfitted with the supplies, tools, and animals for the long, hard journey that was ahead of them. Do you know what they had to do after they joined a wagon train and packed their supplies? They had to wait on one more thing."

"I know, Dad," Molly said. "They had to wait for the grass to turn green so that they could feed the horses, oxen, and other animals along the trail."

"You're right, Molly," replied her dad. "Now let's all go inside and learn how to pack our wagons just like the pioneers did for their trip out West."

As we head into the museum to learn how to pack our wagons, let's read God's map and find out what Abram does and where he goes after Pharaoh's men escort him out of the land of Egypt.

Turn to page 161. Read Genesis 13 and mark the following key words:

Abram (color it blue)

Lot (color it orange)

<u>land</u> (double-underline it in green and color it blue)

altar (draw a red box around it)

Don't forget to mark anything that tells you WHERE by double-underlining the <u>WHERE</u> in green. And don't forget to mark anything that tells you WHEN by drawing a green clock like this: 🕐

Now turn back to the map on page 19 and follow Abram's journey as you answer the 5 W's and an H questions.

Genesis 13:1 WHERE did Abram go from Egypt?

_____

The Negev is the wilderness, a parched land. It is the southern district of Judah.

Genesis 13:3 WHERE did Abram journey from the Negev?

_____

Genesis 13:3,4 WHAT did Abram do when he returned to

the place his tent was before?_____

_____

Isn't it awesome to see Abram returning to worship God
and call on His name after he had failed? Abram sinned when
he chose to do things his way instead of trusting God. But
God intervened. He protected Abram and His promise to him.
Once Abram realized his failure, did he give up? No way! Our
brave explorer moves on. He doesn't stay in his failure. He
returns to God to call on His name and worship Him.

Genesis 13:5-7 WHAT is happening in these verses?

_____

_____

_____

Genesis 13:8,9 WHAT does Abram tell Lot to do?

_____

Genesis 13:10,11 WHAT land did Lot choose?

_____

Genesis 13:13 WHAT do we see about the men of Sodom
where Lot settled?

_____

Genesis 13:12 WHERE did Abram settle?

_____

Genesis 13:14,15 WHAT did the Lord tell Abram after he and Lot separated?

_____

_____

Genesis 13:16 WHAT did God tell Abram about his descendants?

_____

Genesis 13:17 WHAT did God tell Abram to do?

_____

Genesis 13:18 WHERE did Abram move his tent?

_____

Genesis 13:18 WHAT did Abram do?

_____

Did you notice the conflict between Lot and Abram? Abram's character is revealed as we see him allowing Lot to choose the land he wanted first. Abram was rich, but he was not greedy. Did you notice that Lot chose what he thought was the best land? Was it?

Have you ever had to share the last piece of cake with your brother or sister? When you cut the cake, did you choose the best piece for yourself, or did you allow your brother or sister to choose first?

———————————————

Remember, God watches what we do and rewards our unselfishness.

What did God show Abram after he finally separated from Lot? For the first time God shows Abram the land that He has promised him. Wow! Then God tells him that this land will belong to his descendants forever.

He also tells him that he is going to have so many descendants that they will not be able to be numbered. Isn't that amazing, since Abram is 75 years old and doesn't even have one child? Yet, God is promising him that one day he will have so many descendants that he won't be able to count them all!

Today we have also seen two very different choices: Lot chose what he thought was the best land, but Abram waited on God to show him the land He had promised. How do these choices affect these two men's lives? We'll find out as we continue our journey.

HOW about you? Do you make choices without God's help, or do you wait on God to show you what is best?

Write out what you do.

———————————————

Now that our wagons are packed, let's head to the courthouse in Independence, Missouri, and jump off on the Oregon Trail while we practice saying our memory verse out loud. Westward ho! Let's go!

GOD'S EXPLORER MEETS THE KINGS

"All right!" Max shouted as his whole family piled into the SUV and left Independence. "Westward ho! We are finally on the Oregon Trail! Hey, Molly, did you know that as the pioneers crossed the Missouri border they were also leaving the United States?"

"Hey," replied Molly, "that's kind of like Abram leaving his country to follow God's call."

"It sure is," said Max. "As the wagon master gave the order 'Wagons, ho!' the wagons would creak their way across the plains, leaving the United States on a five- to six-month journey that would change their lives forever."

"I sure am glad it isn't going to take us five to six months to get to Oregon," joined in Max's mom.

Everyone laughed. Max's mom said, "Now why don't we pull out God's map as we hit the trail. Let's head back to Genesis to follow our brave explorer and watch how his journey of following God changes his life."

Are you ready to hit the trail? Have you prayed? Great! Then pull out God's map and turn to page 162. Read Genesis 14 and mark the following key words:

God (draw a purple triangle and color it yellow)

bless (blessing, blessed) (put a blue cloud around it an color it pink)

Abram (color it blue)

Lot (color it orange)

Melchizedek (draw a purple box around it)

Don't forget to mark anything that tells you WHERE by double-underlining the WHERE in green. And don't forget to mark anything that tells you WHEN by drawing a green clock like this:

Now WHAT has happened since Lot and Abram separated? Let's find out by asking the 5 W's and an H.

Genesis 14:1-10 WHAT is happening with these kings? WHAT are they doing? They are at __ __ __ with each other. (awr) (Unscramble the word and place it in the blanks.)

Genesis 14:11 WHAT do they take from Sodom and Gomorrah?

_____

Genesis 14:12 WHAT happens to Lot?

_____

Genesis 14:13-16 WHAT does Abram do when he finds out?

_____

_____

Genesis 14:17 WHAT happens after Abram returns?

_____

Genesis 14:18 WHO comes out to meet him?

_____

Genesis 14:18 WHO is Melchizedek? That's quite a name, isn't it? It's pronounced like this: mel-kee'-zeh-dek.

_____

Genesis 14:19 WHAT does Melchizedek do?

_____

Genesis 14:19 HOW does Melchizedek describe God?

_____

_____

Wow! Isn't that awesome? God's name is *El Elyon,* God Most High. This name means that God is sovereign. He is the One in control. He is the Possessor of heaven and earth. God is the Ruler over all!

Look at Genesis 14:20. WHAT else has God Most High done?

_____

WHAT did Abram give Melchizedek?

_____

Genesis 14:21 WHAT did the king of Sodom want to give Abram?

_____

Genesis 14:22-24 Did Abram take them? WHY or WHY not?

_____

_____

Just look at all we have discovered about our explorer! When Abram hears that his nephew Lot has been taken captive, he goes and rescues him. Abram is victorious in his battle against the kings!

Did you know that God uses conflicts (hard situations) to develop our character and to test our faith? Abram was victorious in his battle, but HOW would he handle his victory?

Would he take the glory for the victory, or would he give the glory to whom it belonged—God?

WHAT does it mean to give God the glory? Have you ever seen a soccer game when someone scored the winning goal? Did the soccer player take the credit for winning the game, or did he share the credit with his entire team? WHO should get the credit: the one who kicked the goal, or the other team members who helped the kicker make the goal?

So WHO should receive the credit for Abram's battle against the kings: Abram or God, who is the Ruler over all and made it happen?

WHAT did Abram do when the king of Sodom tried to give him the goods? He refused. Isn't that awesome? Would you have refused those riches in order to honor God?

Abram refused because he didn't want the king to be able to say he had made Abram rich. Abram gave God the glory. He recognized that not only had God given him victory in the battle against the kings, but He had also given him everything he had. He knew God as God Most High, Possessor of heaven and earth. Just look at how our brave explorer has grown in his relationship with God.

- Do you recognize that God is the Giver of all that you have? _____ Yes _____ No

- Do you recognize that God is the One in control of all your circumstances, even when there is hardship and conflict? _____ Yes _____ No

- Do you give God all the glory for the things that you have and all of your accomplishments? Or do you take the credit for yourself and say, "Look at what I can do"? Write out what you do.

_____

Why don't you take a few minutes and just praise God for WHO He is and what you have learned about Him. Write out a short prayer of praise on the lines below so that you can grow in your journey of faith as you learn how to walk with God.

_____

_____

_____

_____

Now say your verse out loud to your parents or a grown-up. Fantastic! You are becoming quite an explorer!

2

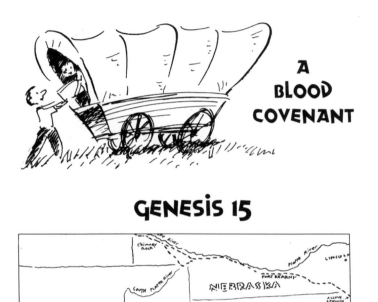

A BLOOD COVENANT

GENESIS 15

"Wow, just look at all those fields!" exclaimed Molly as the SUV headed down the highway. "I have never seen so many fields in all my life."

"Me either," replied Max. "No wonder the pioneers talked about heading out into the wilderness. There still isn't much out here even today. How much longer until we get to Nebraska, Dad?"

"It's coming up, Max. We are about to cross the state line. Then we'll head northwest as we follow the Little Blue River to meet up with the Platte."

"Here we go, Max. There's the state line. We are in Nebraska!" Molly cheered.

"Great. I'm ready to go camping," replied Max.

Max's dad replied, "Hang on, buddy. We still have some driving to do before we arrive at Fort Kearny's park. Did you know that the pioneers only traveled around 15 miles a day? By the time we arrive in Kearney from Independence, we will have traveled around 394 miles."

"Wow! Will we only travel 15 miles a day while we are on our wagon train, Uncle Luke?" Molly asked.

"Yes," replied Max's dad, "but that's still a few days away. Today we will camp near Fort Kearny and spend a couple of days fishing, swimming, boating, and checking out all the historical sites."

"We can't wait!" Molly and Max replied as Sam barked his agreement.

CAMPING WITH GOD

As we head toward Fort Kearny and Sam enjoys his adventure of hanging his head out the window of the SUV, we need to get back to our adventure with God's brave explorer. Let's find out what is happening with Abram since his victorious battle against the kings.

Pull out God's map with Max and Molly and turn to page 165. But don't forget to check in with your Wagon Master before you hit the trail!

Now read Genesis 15 and mark the following key words:

Abram (color it blue)

covenant (draw a yellow box around it and color it red)

land (double-underline it in green and color it blue)

Don't forget to mark anything that tells you WHERE by double-underlining the WHERE in green. And don't forget to mark anything that tells you WHEN by drawing a green clock like this: 🕐

Your map is looking great! Now let's get the facts.

Genesis 15:1 WHEN did the Lord come to Abram in a vision?

After _____ _____

This means that God comes to Abram sometime after his battle with the four kings and reveals Himself to Abram.

Genesis 15:1 WHAT does God say to Abram?

_____

Genesis 15:1 HOW does God reveal Himself to Abram?

"I am a _____ to you; your

_____ shall be very _____."

Isn't that awesome? God shows Abram that he doesn't have to be afraid because He is his protector, his shield. Do you remember how Abram turned down the king of Sodom's reward in order to honor God? Now we see God telling Abram that his reward will be very great. God always blesses us when we put Him first. We don't always see it right away, and neither did Abram. But he will—just wait and see.

Genesis 15:2,3 WHAT is Abram's response?

"O Lord GOD, what will You _____ _____, since

I am _____, and the _____ of my

house is Eliezer of Damascus?"

Genesis 15:4 WHAT does God tell Abram about his heir?
An heir is the person who inherits (receives) the other
person's possessions when he dies.

_____

_____

Genesis 15:5 WHAT does God promise Abram as He
takes him outside to look at the stars?

_____

_____

Genesis 15:6 WHAT was Abram's response?

_____

_____

   Wow! We see in verse 5 that God promises Abram descendants (seed), and Abram believes God and it makes him righteous. Being righteous means to be made right with God.
   Let's find out what Abram believed about the descendants
(the seed) that made him right with God. Look up and read
Galatians 3:16.

To WHOM were the promises spoken?

_____ and his _____

Does this mean many seeds, or is it only one?

_____

WHO is this seed? C __ __ __ __ __

Amazing! Do you see what Abram believed in Genesis 15:6? Abram believed that God would give him a seed, and that seed would be Christ. HOW do we know? Look up and read John 8:56.

WHO is speaking? _____

(If you aren't sure, look back at John 8:54 to see who is speaking.)

John 8:56 WHOSE day did Abraham rejoice to see?

_____ day

WHO is this "My"? WHO did we see was speaking?

_____

Isn't this awesome? Jesus tells us in John 8:56 that Abraham rejoiced to see His (Jesus') day! Abraham was glad! He understood God was promising him Christ when God promised him a seed. Genesis 15:6 shows us Abram's salvation. Abram had faith. He was made right with God because he trusted in God's promise of a seed (Christ).

Now go back to Genesis 15 on page 165.

Genesis 15:7 WHAT does God promise Abram?

_____

Genesis 15:8 WHAT is Abram's question to God?

_____

Genesis 15:9 WHAT does God tell Abram to do?

"Bring Me a _____ year old _____, and a

_____ year old _____ _____, and a

_____ year old _____, and a

_____, and a young

_____."

Genesis 15:10 WHAT did Abram do?

_____

_____

Genesis 15:12 WHAT happened when the sun went down?

_____

Genesis 15:13-16 WHAT did God tell Abram would happen for certain in the future? WHAT was God's prophecy?

Genesis 15:13 "Your _____ will be

_____ in a land that is not theirs, where

they will be _____ and

_____ _____ hundred years."

Genesis 15:14 "I will also _____ the

_____ whom they will serve, and afterward they

will come out with many _____."

Genesis 15:15 "You shall go to your _____ in

_____; you will be _____ at a good old age."

Genesis 15:16 "In the _____ generation they

will _____ here, for the iniquity of the

Amorite is not yet complete."

Genesis 15:17 WHAT happened when the sun had set?

"There appeared a _____ _____

and a _____ _____ which

_____ between these _____."

WHO is this
smoking oven
and flaming torch
that passes
between these
pieces? We know
it's not Abram
because he is in a
deep sleep.

Look at Genesis 15:18. WHO is making the covenant with
Abram?

So if Abram is asleep, WHO appears as a smoking oven

and flaming torch?_____

Genesis 15:18 WHAT two things did God promise Abram
in this covenant?

d __ __ __ __ __ __ __ __ __ s and a l __ __ d

Genesis 15:18 WHAT are the boundaries for this land?

From the _____ of _____ as far as the

great _____, the _____

_____

Great work! You have just discovered something very, very
important—covenant. WHY is covenant important? It's
because everything God does is based on covenant. Do you
know what covenant is? It's a little bit bloody, but it's awesome! We'll find out tomorrow.

Now that we have arrived in Fort Kearny and have set up
our camp, let's sit outside with Max, Molly, and Sam to toast
marshmallows for our s'mores. Take a look at the night sky.
Have you ever seen so many beautiful stars?

As you look at the stars, let's discover your memory verse
for this week. Look at the picture on the next page. Each star
in the picture has a word from your verse that has
been mixed up. Unscramble the letters inside each
star to figure out what the word is. Then place the
word on the blanks underneath the picture. After
you have unscrambled your verse, take a look
at Genesis 15 to discover the reference for this
verse.

Then practice saying your verse aloud
three times in a row. But be careful—as
you practice your verse out loud, Sam is
liable to jump up and take off with your
s'more! You know how he loves to eat!

_____ ____ __ _____ ____ ____ _____

_____; ___ _ ___ _____

____ ___ ___ ___ _____.

—Genesis 15: _____

COVENANT

Good morning! Did you have a good night's sleep? Are you ready to try out one of the pioneers' johnnycakes for breakfast? Good. Then let's get started. Take a look at the pioneers' recipe. You need one pint of milk, three pints of corn meal, and one half pint of flour. Why don't you scald the milk over the fire so Max can mix it with the cornmeal and flour? Then Molly can bake it on the fire.[1]

So what did you think? Pretty different from what you're used to, isn't it? Good thing Max's mom and Aunt Kathy made eggs and bacon, too!

Now that we have eaten, let's head back to our adventure with Abram and discover what a covenant is. Did you know that the Old Testament where the Book of Genesis is found was written in Hebrew? The Hebrew word for *covenant* is *beriyth,* and it is pronounced ber-éeth.

A covenant is a solemn, binding agreement made by passing through pieces of flesh. It is a treaty, an alliance, a pledge, or an agreement. A covenant is a lifelong promise that can never be broken.

The first time God uses the word *covenant* in the Bible is in Genesis 6 with Noah. In Genesis 6 we see God making a covenant with Noah, promising to keep Noah and his family safe during the flood.

In Genesis 9 we see God establishing a covenant with Noah and all flesh, promising to never again send a flood to destroy the entire earth. God gave Noah a sign to remind him of His promise. Do you remember the sign of the covenant that God gave Noah and every living creature? You're right—it was a

---

1. Kristina Gregory, *Dear America Across the Wide and Lonesome Prairie* (New York: Scholastic Inc., 1997), p. 159.

bow in the clouds, a rainbow. Let's draw the sign of God's first covenant in the box below.

Sign of God's First Covenant

Now in Genesis 15 we see God cutting covenant with Abram by telling Abram to bring a three-year-old heifer, a three-year-old female goat, a three-year-old ram, a turtledove, and a young pigeon.

Abram cuts the animals in half, but he doesn't cut the birds. Then he falls into a deep sleep, and God tells him what will happen in the future. Next we see a smoking oven and a flaming torch pass through those pieces of flesh. Do you remember WHO appears as this smoking oven and flaming torch? Look and see WHO passes through the pieces. Was it Abram or God? _____

So WHO made the covenant? _____

God is cutting covenant with Abram. He passes through these pieces of flesh, making a solemn, binding agreement with Abram. WHAT was His promise to Abram?

d _ _ _ _ _ _ _ _ _ _ s and a l _ _ d

This covenant is called the Abrahamic covenant. God made the covenant. It is based on His Word and character. All Abram did was believe. WHY don't you draw a picture below of God cutting this covenant with Abram to help you remember it? Show Abram asleep on the ground as a smoking oven and a flaming torch pass through these pieces of flesh. God was promising Abram descendants and a land forever.

Abrahamic Covenant

Now that we know what a covenant is, let's take a closer look at the prophecy that God gives Abram concerning his descendants. WHAT was God's prophecy in Genesis 15:12-14? Write what God said would happen in Genesis 15:12-14 on the left side of the chart on the next page.

God's Prophecy

Genesis 15:13—"Your_____
_____
will be _____
in a land that is not theirs."

Genesis 15:13—"They will be
_____ and
_____
_____ hundred years."

Genesis 15:14—"I will also
_____ the
_____ whom they
will serve, and afterward they will
come out with many
_____."

The Fullfillment of the Prophecy

Exodus 1:7—The sons of Israel
were_____, increased
greatly, and_____ so
that the land was filled with them.

Exodus 1:8—They are in
E __ __ __ t. Is this their land
that God promised them?____

Exodus 1:11—The Egyptians
appointed taskmasters over them
to _____ them with
hard labor.

Exodus 2:23—The sons of Israel
sighed because of their
_____ , and they
_____ out.

Exodus 2:24—God _____
their groaning, and God
_____ His
_____ with
Abraham, Isaac, and Jacob.

Exodus 12:40,41—The sons of
Israel lived in Egypt _____
hundred and _____
years. (*They were only slaves 400
years because during the first 30
years Joseph was alive, and they
were not slaves during his years.)

Exodus 12:35—The sons of Israel
requested from the Egyptians
articles of _____ and
articles of _____ and
_____.

Exodus 12:36—The Lord gave the
people _____ in the sight
of the _____. Thus
they _____ the
Egyptians.

Now did this prophecy come true? Let's find out by doing some cross-referencing.

Look up and read Exodus 1:1-14 and fill in the right-hand side of the chart that goes with these verses.

Now look up and read Exodus 2:22-25 and fill in the right-hand side of the chart that goes with these verses.

To complete your chart, look up and read Exodus 12:33-41 and fill in the blanks that go with these verses.

Now that we have checked out other passages in the Bible, did the prophecy that God gave Abram come true? It sure did! We have seen how Abram's descendants were enslaved and oppressed and how God brings them out with many possessions. WHAT an awesome God! He is faithful to His covenant. He always keeps His promises!

Now grab your fishing pole and race Max and Molly to the lake to catch your lunch as you sit on the bank to fish and practice your memory verse!

GOD'S COVENANT OF LAW

Wow! That fish you caught yesterday was quite a whopper. It made one great lunch! Pile into the SUV as we head to Fort Kearny. Fort Kearny was built in 1848 to protect the pioneers who traveled the Oregon Trail. It was one of six major forts they would pass on the way west, but it was the only one that was built specifically for their safety.

"We're here!" yelled Max as he opened the door and climbed out of the SUV. "Can we go inside the old fort first?"

"Sure," replied his mom, "but make sure that you stay on the paths. There is a lot of wildlife around, and we need to be careful."

As Max, Molly, and Sam headed to the fort, suddenly Sam shot off, running and barking wildly. "Oh, no," Max's mom called out. "I think Sam has discovered something. You had better catch him, Max!"

"I will, Mom. Sam, come back here, boy. Don't chase that bunny! Sammmmmmm!"

"Whew! That was quite a chase," Max sighed as he carried Sam back toward the rest of the family. "You nearly scared that poor bunny to death. Bad dog! Now you are going to have to stay on your leash while we check out the fort and the blacksmith's shop."

"Hey," Molly cried out, "look at this. This brochure says we can try on some of the old pioneer clothing in the Visitors Center. Then we can go out next to the wagons and have our picture made. Can we do that, Mom?"

"Sure," replied Molly's mom. "Let's all do it together after we check out the fort and old buildings. We can get a family picture of our great adventure. Maybe we'll even put a hat on Sam. I just bet he would love that!" Everyone laughed as they headed toward the old fort.

Now that Sam is on his leash, let's head back to our adventure with Abram. Yesterday we took a closer look at God's covenant with Abram. Today we need to pull out God's map to discover what the next covenant is that God made.

Do you remember WHAT God gave Moses on Mount Sinai? If you don't remember, look up Exodus 20 to find out. Write it out below.

The T__ n C __ __ __ __ __ __ __ __ __ __ s

Now look up and read Exodus 24. This covenant is called the Mosaic covenant or the Law. It is also called the old covenant, and it is given after Moses and the sons of Israel have been rescued from the land of Egypt and now are at Mount Sinai.

Looking at Exodus 24, ask the 5 W's and an H to solve the crossword puzzle on the next page.

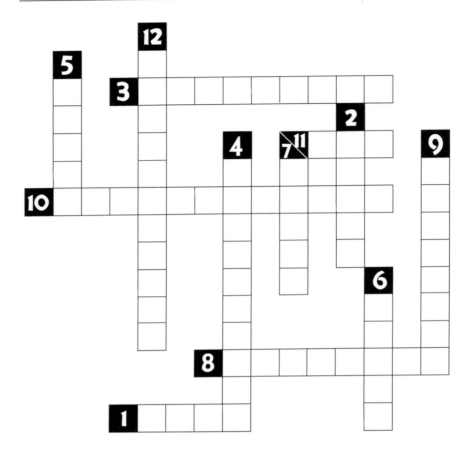

Exodus 24:4 WHAT did Moses do?

1. (Across) He wrote down all the words of the _____.

2. (Down) He built an _____ at the foot of the mountain with 12 pillars for the 12 tribes of Israel.

Exodus 24:5 WHAT did he send the young men to do?

3. (Across) To offer burnt _____.

4. (Down) They _____ young

5. (Down) _____ as 6. (Down) _____ offerings to the Lord.

Exodus 24:6 WHAT did Moses put in basins and sprinkle on the altar?

7. (Down) The _____

Exodus 24:7 WHAT did Moses read in the hearing of the people?

8. (Across) The book of the _____

Exodus 24:7 HOW did the people respond?

9. (Down) "All that the Lord has spoken we will do, and we will be _____!"

Exodus 24:12 WHAT did God tell Moses He would give him?

10. (Across) The _____ _____ (put these two words together) with the 11. (Across) _____ and the 12. (Down) _____ which I have written for their instruction.

Way to go! Now draw a picture of this covenant of law, the old covenant, below. Show Moses with the tablets of stone on Mount Sinai.

Old Covenant (Law)

Great artwork! Let's head back to our campsite to cook some dinner. Tomorrow we will discover more about our faithful God's covenants.

A NEW COVENANT

"Wake up, Max," called his mom at the break of day.

"Oh, do I have to get up, Mom?" Max asked as he cracked open his eyes. "The sun is just now coming up."

"Yes, you do. Dad and Uncle Kyle want to have a sunrise breakfast. Then we need to break camp and head for the Archway Monument museum to get a close-up look at the pioneers' journey."

"Okay, Mom, I'm coming. Sam and I sure will miss Fort Kearny, but we're ready for our next adventure."

How about you? Are you ready to get back on the trail and discover God's new covenant? Spend some time with your Wagon Master, and then let's move out. Pull out God's map and turn to Exodus 24. Let's get started by reading Exodus 24 and writing what we learn about the old covenant on the left side of the chart on the next page.

Old Covenant (the Law)	**New Covenant**
Exodus 24:12—The old covenant was written on s _ _ _ _ e t_ _ _ _ _ _s (Draw a picture of this at the top of this box above the words Old Covenant.)	Jeremiah 31:33—"I will put My _____ _____ them and on their _____ I will write it."
Exodus 24:12 —"...the stone _____ with the _____ and the commandment which I have written for their _____."	Jeremiah 31:34—"I will _____their _____ , and their _____ I will remember no more."
The old covenant shows us our ___ ___ ___ . (ins) (Unscramble this word and place it in the blanks.)	The new covenant forgives our ___ ___ ___. (ins)

Now read Jeremiah 31:31-34 printed out below and mark the following key words:

covenant (draw a yellow box around it and color it red)

law (draw black tablets)

heart (draw a red heart)

Jeremiah 31:31-34:

31"Behold, days are coming," declares the LORD, "when I will make a new covenant with the house of Israel and with the house of Judah, 32 not like the covenant which I made with their fathers in the day I took them by the hand to bring them out of the land of Egypt, My covenant which they broke, although I was a husband to them," declares the LORD. 33 "But this is the covenant which I will make with the house of Israel after those days," declares the LORD, "I will put My law within them and on their heart I will write it; and I will be their God, and they shall be My people. 34 They will not teach again, each man his neighbor and each man his brother, saying, 'Know the LORD,' for they will all know Me, from the least of them to the greatest of them," declares the LORD, "for I will forgive their iniquity, and their sin I will remember no more."

Before God disciplines His people and drives them out of the land for breaking the old covenant, He gives them a promise of the new covenant. Let's look at this covenant and see what we can learn. Look back at the passage in Jeremiah you just marked on page 56 to answer the 5 W's and an H questions below.

Jeremiah 31:31 WHAT is God going to do?

Make a _____ _____ with the house of Israel and the house of Judah

Jeremiah 31:32 Is this the same covenant as the old covenant, the covenant of law? ____ Yes ____ No

Jeremiah 31:33 WHAT will God do with this new covenant—write it on stone tablets? ____ Yes ____ No

Now that we have discovered this new covenant, let's compare it to the old covenant by filling in the right-hand side of our chart on page 55.

Did you see HOW God gave us the law, the old covenant, for instruction? The law was given to show us what sin is. How can we know we are sinners if we don't have a standard to measure ourselves to?

The law was like a teacher to teach us what is right and wrong, to tell us what we could and could not do. It was our standard to show us our sin. But WHAT did we see about the new covenant? WHAT would God do with our sins?
F __ __ __ __ __ e our sins.

Isn't that awesome? But HOW? We'll find out tomorrow as we continue to take a look at the new covenant and the mystery of the torn veil to discover how this covenant can take away our sins.

Now climb back into the SUV. It's time to continue our journey as we leave Fort Kearny and head toward Bayard, Nebraska. Don't forget to practice your memory verse!

THE MYSTERY OF THE TORN VEIL

As the SUV headed down the road, Molly said, "I liked that museum. Those headphones were so cool!"

"My favorite part was the herd of buffalo that came charging at us. That was really awesome," stated Max. "The buffalo jerky was pretty good, too!"

"I'm so glad I didn't live back then," Molly replied. "Imagine having to collect buffalo patties when the firewood was scarce so that you could cook and have heat. That is really gross!"

"I liked how they said the boys would throw the buffalo chips at each other. Now that's a cool game!"

"Yuck!" Molly responded. "Where are we headed next, Mom?"

"Our next big stop will probably be Windlass Hill and Ash Hollow," answered Molly's mom. "So why don't you guys pull out God's map to find out about the new covenant and the mystery of the torn veil?"

How about you? Are you ready to discover more about God's new covenant and uncover a mystery? Then spend some time talking to God. Pull out God's map and look up and read Matthew 26:26-29.

Now uncover the mystery.

Matthew 26:27-28 WHAT did Jesus say as He gave thanks and gave them the cup to drink?

"Drink from it, all of you; for this is My _____ of

the _____, which is poured out for many for

_____ of _____."

Do you remember which covenant was for the forgiveness of sins? Write it out: The _____ covenant

Let's look up and read Matthew 27:26-54.

Matthew 27:26 WHAT did they do to Jesus?

_____

Matthew 27:43 WHO did Jesus say He was?

_____

Matthew 27:50 WHAT happened?

_____

Matthew 27:51 WHAT happened to the veil in the temple when Jesus died?

_____

Amazing! Did you know that the veil in the temple was so thick and heavy it would have taken two teams of horses pulling in opposite directions to be able to tear this veil in two?

Let's find out more about the mystery of this veil. Turn to Hebrews 10 and read verses 9-22.

Hebrews 10:9 This "He" is Jesus speaking. WHAT did He come to do?

_____

Hebrews 10:9 WHAT was taken away? The f _ _ _ t

Do you know what this "first" was? HOW about the old covenant? WHEN it was taken away, WHAT was established?

The s _ _ _ _ d

WHAT do you think this is?

_____

Hebrews 10:10 HOW have we been sanctified? *Sanctified* means "to be made clean, to be set apart." HOW are we made clean, forgiven of our sins?

Through the offering of the _____ of _____

_____ _____ for _____

HOW was Jesus' body offered as a sacrifice? WHAT did we see in Matthew 27:35? WHAT did they do to Jesus?

They c _ _ _ _ _ _ _ d Him.

Look at Hebrews 10:16,17. These are the same verses we read about the new covenant in Jeremiah 31 yesterday. Remember how we saw that the new covenant would take away our sins? HOW did we just see in Hebrews 10:10 that we are made clean and forgiven of our sins?

_____

Let's look at Hebrews 10:19. HOW do we have confidence to enter the holy place?

_____

Hebrews 10:20 WHAT is the new and living way (the new covenant) that Jesus inaugurated for us?

Through the _____

And WHAT is the mystery of the veil? WHAT does the veil represent?

Jesus' _____

Now let's take a look inside the tabernacle by making our own tabernacle. Get a shoe box and cut a door in the center of the end so that you have an opening. Draw a picture of the bronze altar on the shoe box as you first come through the "door." Next draw a picture of the bronze laver.

You need a handkerchief to hang as a curtain. You can color this handkerchief brown with colored markers. After you color it, hang it from one side of the shoebox to the other and staple it there.

Inside the curtain you need to draw a lampstand on the left and the table of showbread on the right, and in the middle you need to draw the altar of incense (see p. 62).

Now get another handkerchief and color it blue, red, and purple to represent the veil in the tabernacle, and then hang it right behind the altar of incense. Behind the veil draw the mercy seat on the ark of the covenant, and in front of it write "Holy of Holies," just like in the picture.

Now let's take a closer look at the tabernacle.

The mercy seat was a picture of God's throne, and only the high priest could enter the holy of holies once a year to sprinkle blood on the mercy seat for sin. But WHAT does Matthew 27:51 tell you happened to the veil when Jesus, our High Priest, died on the cross?

_____

WHAT was this torn veil a picture of?

_____

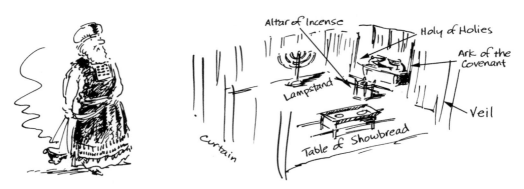

The torn veil showed that Jesus' death on the cross paid for all our sins. Now anyone who believes in Jesus and is saved can come directly to God Himself, instead of through the priest. This is grace—the unearned favor for every child of the new covenant.

Look up and read John 14:6.

WHAT is Jesus?

_____

WHAT is the only way to the Father?

_____

Salvation is by faith through the new covenant. It is not by keeping the law or doing good deeds. The only way we can be forgiven of our sins is to believe in Jesus and accept Him as our Savior. Now look up and read Ephesians 3:14-16.

Ephesians 3:16 HOW does God strengthen us with His power?

Through His _____ in the _____ man

God puts His Spirit within us. Isn't that awesome!

Jesus' death on the cross, the new covenant, is the only way we can be forgiven of our sins and receive the Holy Spirit who gives us power over sin.

Draw a picture of the new covenant in the box below. WHAT should you draw? WHAT did Jesus do to pay for our sins? Show Jesus shedding His blood by being crucified on a cross to pay for our sins.

Now go back to page 55 and draw a picture of the cross in the box over the heading "New Covenant."

New Covenant

How about you? Have you entered into the new covenant with God? Have you received God's gift of salvation? We have seen that faith in Jesus is the only way to be saved. We can never be good enough. We cannot earn our salvation. It is a gift from God when we believe in His Son, Jesus Christ.

If you haven't received God's gift of salvation, then all you need to do is go to God and tell Him that you want to be saved. Tell Him that you are a sinner (Romans 3:23—"For all have sinned and fall short of the glory of God"), that you are sorry for your sins, and that you want to be a follower of Jesus Christ.

You can pray a prayer like this:

> *Thank You, God, for loving me and sending Your Son, Jesus Christ, to die for my sins. I am sorry for the things I have done wrong. I am repenting, changing my mind about my sins. Sin is wrong. I don't want to do things my way anymore. I want to receive Jesus Christ as my Savior, and now I turn my entire life over to You. Amen.*

God has forgiven all of your sins and will send His Spirit to live in you (John 14:23)! You can walk in God's ways because you have His Spirit inside you to help you do what God says is right.

> *Therefore if anyone is in Christ, he is a new creature; the old things passed away; behold, new things have come* (2 Corinthians 5:17).

3

ABRAM'S NEW NAME

GENESIS 16–18

"Okay, guys, are you ready to stop?" asked Max's mom.

"We sure are," replied Max. "Sam is about to croak. He's ready to get out."

"You need to make sure that you, Molly, and Sam all stay on the path while you're here," said Max's dad. "This is rattlesnake country, and you need to be very careful."

"Okay, Dad. Is this Windlass Hill?"

"Yes it is," replied Max's Aunt Kathy. "And right over there is Ash Hollow, one of the most favored spots of the pioneers along the trail where they could find shade trees, firewood, and lots of grass for their animals, and some of the best drinking water around.

"But before they could get to Ash Hollow, they had to go down one of the steepest descents ever: Windlass Hill. It was so steep and the drop so terrifying that some of the emigrants would travel 17 miles out of their way just to avoid it."

"Wow!" exclaimed Molly. "Can we climb to the top?"

"Yes, you can," replied her mom. "Go ahead and get out. Just be careful and wait for us at the top. This is one of the best spots to see the original wagon ruts made by the pioneers."

"Awesome!" exclaimed Max. "Let's go! Come on, Sam!"

HELPING GOD OUT

"Wow, just look!" Molly cried out. "Look at all those hills and valleys. How did the pioneers ever drive those wagons over such steep and rough terrain? Are those the wagon ruts, Mom?"

"Yes, just look at all those trails across the plains. Now look this way. Look straight down into that ravine. We are standing right over the steep hill I was telling you about where a lot of pioneers broke their wagons and their bones."

"Boy, it is really amazing how they survived such a long, hard journey," Max said.

"Many of them didn't, Max," replied Max's mom, Jena. "With the rough terrain, the weather, sickness, and rattlesnake bites, there were a lot of graves along the way. Let's head down to the bottom and check out the little sod house.

"Then, we need to find out what is happening with our brave explorer since God made His covenant promise with him."

So, brave explorers, are you ready to continue our journey? Spend some time with your Wagon Master, then turn to page 166 and read Genesis 16. Mark the following key words:

God (draw a purple triangle and color it yellow)

Abram (color it blue)

Sarai (color it pink)

Hagar (color it orange)

Don't forget to mark anything that tells you WHERE by double-underlining the <u><u>WHERE</u></u> in green. And don't forget to mark anything that tells you WHEN by drawing a green clock like this:

Now let's do a quick review. Let's read Genesis 12:1-3 on page 159.

Genesis 12:3 WHAT does God promise Abram?

"In you all the _____ of the _____ will be blessed."

WHAT has to happen for Abram to have a family of his own?

_____

Look back at Genesis 11:30 on page 159.

WHAT do we see about Abram's wife, Sarai?

_____

Read Genesis 15:1-4 on page 165. WHAT is Abram's solution to this problem of not having a child and an heir?

Genesis 15:2 WHOM does Abram tell God could be his heir?

"The heir of my house is _____ of_____."

Genesis 15:4 HOW does God respond to Abram's suggestion?

_____

Genesis 15:4 WHOM does God say will be Abram's heir?

"One who will come forth from _____ _____

_____."

Now turn back to page 166 to Genesis 16 and read verses 1-3.

Genesis 16:2 WHAT is Sarai's solution?

_____

Now think a minute. Does God need Abram and Sarai's help in order to keep His promise of giving them so many descendants they can't be counted? No way!

- Have you ever tried to help God out by doing things your way instead of waiting on Him? ___ Yes ___ No Write out what you did on the lines below.

_____

_____

_____

Now let's discover this week's memory verse by solving the rebus on the next page. A rebus is a word puzzle that mixes pictures and words. When you combine the pictures and the letters by adding or subtracting letters, you will end up with a new word.

So as you solve the rebus, write it out on the lines underneath the picture. Then find the reference that goes with this verse. (Hint: The first portion of this verse is missing.)

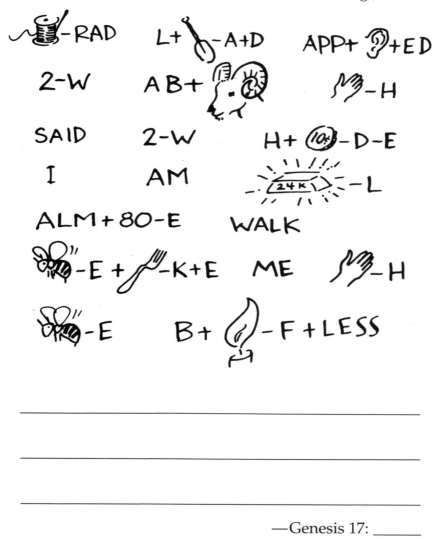

_____

_____

_____

—Genesis 17: _____

You did it! Now practice saying this verse out loud three times in a row, three times today! Tomorrow as we continue to follow our brave explorer, we will find out what can happen when we try to help God out and how much better it is when we just wait on Him!

EL ROI—GOD SEES

"Ash Hollow was pretty neat," Max said as the SUV continued down the highway. "I liked looking at the underground cave."

Max's mom laughed as she said, "You sure love caves, don't you, buddy? Thank goodness this cave was set up for visitors, not like your cave adventure with Uncle Jake."

"I'll never forget that!" Molly added. "I was so scared when Max disappeared. Thank goodness God knew exactly where Max was and led the search team to him!"

"That's right, sweetheart," answered Max's mom. "Even in Max's difficult situation, God was there watching out for him. Why don't we pull out God's map and turn to Genesis 16 to find out what is happening with Abram's difficult situation?"

Okay, brave explorers, let's pray. Now head back to Genesis 16 to find out what happens after Sarai comes up with her idea of how she thinks God will give her a child. Turn to page 166 and read Genesis 16.

Genesis 16:3 WHOM did Sarai give to Abram to become his wife?

_____

Genesis 16:4,5 WHAT happened after Hagar conceived Abram's child? She d ___ ___ ___ ___ ___ ___ d Sarai.

This word *despised* means "to make light of, to be lessened or insignificant." This could mean that once Hagar was pregnant she thought less of Sarai and could have made fun of her or rubbed it in that she was pregnant and Sarai was not.

Have you ever rubbed it in when you had something that someone else didn't have?

_____

Genesis 16:6 HOW did Sarai treat Hagar?

_____

Genesis 16:6 WHAT does Hagar do?

_____

Genesis 16:7 WHO finds Hagar?

_____

Genesis 16:9 WHAT does the angel of the Lord tell her to do?

"_____ to your _____, and

_____ yourself to her_____."

Genesis 16:10 WHAT does the angel of the Lord tell her he will do?

_____

Genesis 16:11,12 WHAT does the angel of the Lord tell her about her child she is pregnant with?

You shall bear a _____.

You shall call his name _____.

He will be a _____ _____ of a man.

His _____ will be against _____,

and everyone's _____ will be against him.

He will live to the _____ of all his

_____.

Genesis 16:13 WHAT does Hagar call the name of the Lord?

"You are a _____ who _____."

Did you know that the Hebrew name for God in this passage is *El Roi?* This means "the God who sees." God saw what happened to Hagar. He knew about her affliction, her pain and distress. God saw her run away, and He sent an angel to let her know that He cared. God loves us. He knows all our circumstances. We cannot run away and hide from Him.

Genesis 16:15 WHAT happens next?

_____

Genesis 16:15 WHAT is his name?

_____

Do you know what Ishmael's name means? It means "God hears." Isn't that awesome? God saw Hagar flee and He heard. He gave heed to her affliction.

We also saw that Ishmael would live to the east of his brothers. Today that would be the Arabs and the Saudis from Saudi Arabia. Do the Israelis have any trouble with the Arabs who live to their east? They sure do. So what God's angel told Hagar is still happening today!

Now go back to page 13 and add Abram's first son and who this son's mother is on the family tree.

Genesis 16:16 HOW old is Abram? _____

Abram was 75 years old when God gave Him the promise of being a great nation. HOW long has it been since God made this promise?

_____

Wow! Abram and Sarai have been waiting a really long time! HOW did we see Sarai handle this long wait? She became impatient and decided to help God out in keeping His promise. She went to Abram and shared her idea of how God might give them their son.

WHAT did Abram do? Did he remind Sarai of who God is? Look at all that Abram knew about God. He knew God as God Most High, a sovereign God who is in control of all our circumstances. And he knew that God is a covenant-keeping God who always keeps His promises. Did he turn to God?

No! Once again we see our brave explorer making a very big mistake! Instead of listening to God, he listens to Sarai. WHAT happens when we listen to man or ourselves instead of God? We have nothing but heartache and trouble!

Just look at Abram's mess! Sarai is upset, she treats Hagar harshly, and Hagar runs away. Do you see how sin affects other people? Abram's mistake affected himself, Sarai, and Hagar, and it will eventually affect their child, as well as their descendants. Remember the Arabs and the Israelis; do they live in peace today? Sin always has consequences. It doesn't just affect us, but it always affects our families and other people too!

Remember, God always knows and does what is best for us. He has a plan for Abram, and when the time is right He will bring it to pass His way—not Abram's or Sarai's.

Did you also notice that even though Abram messed up and Hagar ran away, God saw it all and intervened? Isn't that awesome to know that God is a God who sees all of our mistakes, hurts, and fears?

Sorry...

The next time you sin and make a mistake, remember that God sees and turn to Him. Ask Him to forgive you for your sin and to help you do things His way. Remember, God not only sees but He hears, too! Run to Him and give Him all your cares.

Way to go! Now that we have arrived at our next stop, continue your walk with God as you practice saying your memory verse out loud three times in a row, three times today!

GOD ALMIGHTY

"Look!" exclaimed Molly as she looked out the window. "Look at those huge rocks. Where are we, Uncle Luke?"

"Those rocks are called Courthouse and Jailhouse Rock," replied Uncle Luke. "By this time the pioneers were worn out and bored with the long journey. So as they came across Nebraska and saw these strange rock formations, they became their entertainment.

"Most of the pioneers were Midwesterners who had never seen such huge and strange rock formations. So they would name them and use them for landmarks on their journey to help them know how far they had come and how far they still had to go. They would watch these formations every day until they finally got close enough to stop and climb them."

"All right," Max yelled. "Can we climb them, Dad?"

"Yes, you can. But you have to be careful! Like I said before, this is rattlesnake country, and you have to watch where you step and where you put your hands."

"Okay, we will. Come on, Molly. Let's see if we can beat Sam to the top of Courthouse Rock."

You did it! You made it to the top! What a view! Now let's head back down the trail and find out what is happening with Abram. When we left him yesterday, he was 86 years old and had just had Ishmael with Hagar, Sarai's maid.

Don't forget to pray and then turn to page 168. Read Genesis 17 and mark the following key words:

Abram (Abraham) (color it blue)

covenant (draw a yellow box around it and color it red)

land (double-underline it in green and color it blue)

nations (color it green and underline it in brown)

circumcised (draw a red knife)

bless (draw a blue cloud and color it pink)

descendants (blue star of David)

Don't forget to mark anything that tells you WHERE by double-underlining the WHERE in green. And don't forget to mark anything that tells you WHEN by drawing a green clock like this: 🕐

Way to go! Your map looks fantastic! Tomorrow we will use it as we continue our journey. Did you practice saying your memory verse today?

A SIGN OF THE COVENANT

"Dad," Max asked, "didn't you say that once we saw Courthouse and Jailhouse Rocks we would be close to the ranch where we are joining our wagon train?"

"I sure did, Max. In fact, we'll be there before you know it."

"Yippee!" Max and Molly both yelled at the same time.

Max laughed as he said, "We are going on a real wagon train. This is going to be so cool."

"Hey, Mom," Molly asked, "are you going to ride the horses and drive the wagons?"

"You better believe it! Aunt Jena and I are going to be real pioneer women. Look up ahead, guys. We are about to turn off at the ranch."

As Max and Molly bounced in their seats, Sam felt their excitement and started hopping around, looking out of everybody's window, causing everyone to crack up laughing.

Max's mom said, "I wonder how Sam will take to the wilderness. He will probably run his legs off." Sam turned around just as she finished to give her face a good lick, showing her he agreed with her statement.

"Okay, guys, we're here," Max's dad said as the SUV came to a stop under some shady trees. "It's time to get out and unload our gear. While you help Uncle Kyle, I'll go find Mr. Banyon to let him know that we are here."

Are you excited? It's time to really pack our wagons and head out on a covered wagon adventure like the pioneers. As we start loading up the wagons, don't forget to check in with your Wagon Master—God. Then check out God's map by turning to page 168. Read Genesis 17 and continue your journey.

Genesis 17:1 HOW old is Abram? _____ years old

Abram was 75 years old in Genesis 12:4 when God promised him He would make him a great nation, and now we see he is 99 years old. HOW long has it been since God's promise?

_____ years

Look at Genesis 17:1 as God appears to Abram. WHO does God tell Abram He is? "I am _____ _____."

The Hebrew name for God in this verse is *El Shaddai,* which is translated as "God Almighty." This name of God means just what it says: God is the Almighty One, the powerful or mighty One. Some believe this name also means the all-sufficient One. God is all that we need.

Genesis 17:1 WHAT did God tell Abram to do?

"_____ before Me, and be_____."

That applies to us, too. If we walk the way God wants us to walk, we will be blameless, too! HOW about you? HOW do you walk: God's way or your way?

_____

Genesis 17:2 WHAT is God going to do?

"I will establish My _____ between Me

and you, and I will _____ you exceedingly."

Genesis 17:4 WHAT is God going to make Abram the father of?

A multitude of _____

Genesis 17:5 WHAT does God do in this verse?

He changes Abram's name to _____.

Abram's name meant "exalted father" or "high father." Now God has changed his name to Abraham, which means "father of a multitude." God has promised that kings and nations would come from Abram. Now He changes Abram's name to reflect that promise.

Genesis 17:7 HOW long is this covenant to last?

It is for an _____ covenant.

Genesis 17:8 WHAT is to be given to Abraham and his descendants for an everlasting possession?

All the _____ of _____

Genesis 17:10-11 WHAT is the sign of the covenant that Abraham and his descendants are to keep? WHAT are they to do?

"You shall be _____."

Genesis 17:12 WHO is to be circumcised?

"Every _____ among you who is _____ days old."

Genesis 17:14 WHAT happens to the male who is not circumcised?

"That person shall be _____ _____ from his people." (Circle these two words together on the word search on page 80.)

Genesis 17:14 WHY? "He has _____ My covenant."

If you don't know what circumcision is, ask your parent.

Genesis 17:15 WHOSE name did God change? _____

Genesis 17:15 WHAT is her new name? _____

   Isn't that awesome? God changes Sarai's name to Sarah, which means "princess."

Genesis 17:16 HOW is God going to bless Sarah?

"I will give you a _____ by her."

Genesis 17:17 WHAT did Abraham do?

He fell on his face and _____.

WHY? Because Abraham thinks that he and Sarah are too old to have a child. So in Genesis 17:18 he pleads with God to remember WHOM? _____

Genesis 17:19 WHAT does God say?

"No, but Sarah your wife will bear you a son, and you shall call his name _____."

Genesis 17:19 WHOM is God's covenant going to be through: Ishmael and his descendants or Isaac and his descendants?

_____ and his descendants

Genesis 17:20 Even though the promise isn't through Ishmael and his descendants, we see that God hasn't forgotten him. WHAT is God going to do for him?

I will _____ him, and will make him _____

and will multiply Him exceedingly. He shall become

the father of twelve _____, and I will make

him a great nation.

Genesis 17:22-26 WHEN was Abraham circumcised?

That very same _____

Now find the answers from each one of the blanks of the questions from Genesis 17:1-26 and circle them in the word search below. If a word is used twice, you only need to find it once in the word search.

D	E	R	D	N	U	H	E	N	O	O	W	F	N
L	E	A	M	H	S	I	S	A	A	C	R	A	B
N	V	S	L	A	N	D	E	H	G	U	A	L	C
E	E	N	I	N	E	T	Y	N	I	N	E	O	S
P	R	I	N	C	E	S	I	T	A	S	V	A	B
S	L	U	W	S	M	F	F	C	S	E	R	R	Y
A	A	Y	O	A	K	U	D	T	N	A	O	T	T
R	S	N	L	F	L	A	C	A	H	K	H	E	E
A	T	E	T	P	Y	K	N	R	E	G	K	I	N
I	I	S	N	O	I	T	A	N	I	A	I	K	I
N	N	X	W	Y	G	T	N	M	L	C	N	E	X
H	G	B	L	A	M	E	L	E	S	S	G	O	D
D	A	B	R	A	H	A	M	U	W	A	S	G	Z
C	U	T	O	F	F	T	D	J	M	T	J	J	A

Did you notice as you did your study that God tells Abraham what to do and Abraham obeys immediately?

- Do you obey your parents immediately when they ask you to do something? Or do you argue with them, especially when they ask you to do something you don't want to do? Write out what you do below.

_____

Look at how Abraham responded to God's command of circumcision. This was not an easy command to obey. Circumcision was a very painful thing. But Abraham did not argue or complain. He just simply obeyed God.

Immediately, that very day, Abraham had himself, Ishmael (who was 13 years old), and all the men of his household circumcised, just like God told him to do. The next time your mom or dad ask you to do something, remember Abraham's obedience. Honor them by obeying immediately, without grumbling or complaining. You can do it! Just tell God you want to obey and honor Him.

GOD AND HIS MESSENGERS

As Max and Molly helped unload their sleeping bags and gear from the SUV, Luke, Max's dad, and two other men walked up. "Okay, everyone," Luke said, "I want to introduce you to Mr. Banyon. This is his ranch, and this is his wagon master, Murph. Murph, Mr. Banyon, I want you to meet my wife, Jena, our son, Max, Jena's sister, Kathy, Kathy's husband, Kyle, and their daughter, Molly."

As Luke finished his introductions, Sam started barking. "Oh, I almost forgot. This is the best detective beagle around, Max's dog, Sam. He always keeps us on our toes!" Everybody laughed as Murph reached down to give Sam a pat on his head.

"Well, it's nice to meet you," Murph replied. "I will be your wagon master on this trip. Mr. Banyon will hand out your gear and show you to your wagons while I get the rest of our supplies loaded up. Then we'll grab some lunch before we hit the trail. Are you ready to go?" Everyone cheered, and Murph and Mr. Banyon laughed.

"Okay, head this way, and I will get you set up," Mr. Banyon said, as he led the group toward a small building.

As they walked up to the building, Max and Molly noticed Max's dad wink at his mom.

"What's up, Mom?" Max asked. "I know you two. You're up to something."

Max's mom just smiled, "Oh, we have a little surprise for you and Molly. Dad was just letting me know 'it' had arrived safely."

Max and Molly got excited. "What is it? Can we see it?" Just as they got the questions out of their mouths, they looked up to see their Uncle Jake and Max's Aunt Sherry come out of the building, laughing as they headed their way.

"Uncle Jake, Aunt Sherry, how did you get here?"

"Surprise!" yelled Aunt Sherry. "Jake and I couldn't stand the thought of missing out on a real covered-wagon adventure, so we decided to fly here to join you in your trek across the Nebraska wilderness."

"This is a great surprise!" exclaimed Max. Sam agreed as he ran around jumping up and down, not sure to whom he should give his special licking first.

"Now that everyone is here, let's start packing those wagons," said Mr. Banyon. "These sacks have your enamelware plate and cup, which you get to keep after your trip, some silverware, a rain poncho, and an envelope, paper, and pencil so you can write a letter for the pony express to deliver."

"All right! This is going to be so awesome," exclaimed Max.

Mr. Banyon agreed as he replied, "Now let's go pack those wagons."

While we get ready for our trip into the Nebraska wilderness, let's continue our journey with Abraham.

Pull out God's map and turn to page 170. Read Genesis 18:1-19 and mark the following key words for just these first 19 verses:

Abraham (color it blue)

<u>nations</u> (color it green and underline it in brown)

blessed (draw a blue cloud and color it pink)

Also, when you come to the key phrase *"Is anything too difficult for the LORD?"* mark it by circling it in purple and coloring it orange.

Don't forget to mark anything that tells you WHERE by double-underlining the <u>WHERE</u> in green. And don't forget to mark anything that tells you WHEN by drawing a green clock like this: 🕐

Looking back at Genesis 17:1, HOW old is Abraham?

Abraham is _____ years old.

HOW long has it been since God promised Abraham He would make him a great nation in Genesis 12:1-4?

_____ years

Genesis 18:1 WHAT is happening?

_____

Genesis 18:2-5 WHAT is the main thing happening in these verses?

_____

_____

Genesis 18:1-2 WHO are these three men? Do you know? WHO appears to Abraham by the oaks of Mamre in verse 1? _____

So we see that one of the three is the Lord. Some people believe this is Jesus before He became a baby. Can you figure out who the other two men were? Take a look at Genesis 18:22. The two men departed, heading toward Sodom, leaving the Lord speaking with Abraham. Now look at Genesis 19:1. WHO are the two who arrive in Sodom?

The two a ___ ___ ___ ___ s came to Sodom.

Genesis 18:6-8 WHAT does Abraham do?

_____

_____

Genesis 18:9,10 WHAT did the Lord tell Abraham would happen this time next year?

_____

Genesis 18:11 WHAT do we see about Abraham and Sarah?

_____

So if Abraham is 99 years old in Genesis 17:1, and the Lord tells him he will have a son this time next year, HOW old will Abraham be when this child is born?

_____ years old

Do we know HOW old Sarah will be? Look at Genesis 17:17. We see there is a ten-year age difference between Abraham and Sarah. So HOW old will Sarah be when Isaac is born?

_____ years old

Genesis 18:12 WHAT did Sarah do?

_____

WHY do you think Sarah laughed?

_____

Genesis 18:13,14 WHAT was the Lord's response (we marked it on our Observation Worksheet)?

_____

Genesis 18:15 WHY did Sarah deny laughing?

_____

Genesis 18:16 WHERE were the men looking as Abraham

walked with them?_____

Genesis 18:17 WHAT does the Lord ask?

"Shall I _____ from Abraham what I am about to do?"

Genesis 18:19 WHAT do we see the Lord has done concerning Abraham?

"For I have _____ him, so that he

may_____ his _____ and his

_____ after him to _____ the way

of the_____ by doing _____

and _____."

Now look at all we have learned about our brave explorer today. Abraham is 99 years old, and the Lord comes with two men (angels) to tell him that he will have his son this time next year. Isn't that awesome?

Is anything too difficult for the Lord? No! Remember what you have learned about God. God is an Almighty God, He is in control of all our circumstances, He sees, and He hears. Nothing is too difficult for God!

Now before you head out on your journey, look up and read Romans 4:18-21.

Did you see how Abraham had hope against hope? He knew he was too old to have a child, but God said he would at this time next year, so he chose to believe God.

Will you do like God's brave explorer did? No matter how hard and difficult your circumstances are, will you have hope against hope and believe God? _____ Yes _____ No

Did you notice that Abraham did not waver in unbelief but grew strong in faith, giving glory to WHOM? That's right—God! He knew that what God had promised He was able to perform.

Do you know that about God? Do you believe that God can do anything in spite of how impossible it looks? Do you have an unwavering faith like Abraham's? _____ Yes _____ No

Now why don't you write out a short prayer to God on the lines below, asking Him to help you have a faith like Abraham's, to help you know that nothing is too difficult for Him!

_____

_____

_____

_____

Fantastic! You are on your way to a lifelong journey of growing in your faith!

4

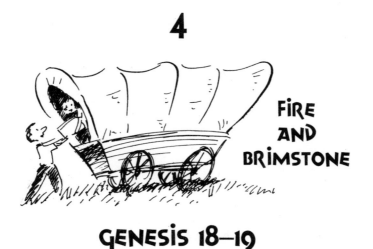

FiRE AND BRiMSTONE

GENESiS 18–19

Are you ready to trek across the Nebraska wilderness to see what it actually felt like to be a pioneer without bathrooms, beds, or kitchens? Great! Then let's join Max, Molly, and Sam as they get their wagons packed for their fun-filled adventure.

ABRAHAM WALKS WiTH GOD

Murph walked up to the picnic area. "Is there anyone here who would like to ride a horse?" he asked with a smile in his voice.

"We do," Molly replied excitedly as she pointed to herself and Max.

"All right, Max, you can ride Half Pint, and Molly can ride Buttermilk. I'll help Jena, Kathy, and Sherry drive their wagon, and Luke, Kyle, and Jake can drive the other wagon. Are you ready to move out?"

"Yes, sir!" Max and Molly yelled as they headed out to mount their horses. Max mounted Half Pint, an Indian

Appaloosa mare, while Molly mounted Buttermilk, Half Pint's sister. Willow, Half Pint's colt, stood next to his mother.

Everyone else climbed into their wagons, with Sam sitting next to Murph on the driver's seat. Once everyone was ready, Murph snapped the reins and called out "Waaagoooonsssss hoooo!" as Chip and Sally, Murph's team of draft horses, started the wagons lumbering across the plains with Max's and Molly's horses trotting behind the rolling wagons. We are on our way!

Now that we are on the move across the plains, let's finish marking God's map on Genesis 18. Turn to page 172. Mark the following key words in Genesis 18:19-33:

Abraham (color it blue)

sin (color it brown)

destroy (draw black squiggly lines)

wicked (color it black)

righteous (color light-blue with an "R")

Don't forget to mark anything that tells you WHERE by double-underlining the <u>WHERE</u> in green. And don't forget to mark anything that tells you WHEN by drawing a green clock like this: 🕐

All right! Let's discover our memory verse by looking at some of Murph's artifacts below. On each one of the pioneers' artifacts there is a number and a letter. Under the artifacts are the blanks from your verse with a number under each blank. Find the letter that matches the number on the artifact and write that letter on the blank to find out what your memory verse is this week.

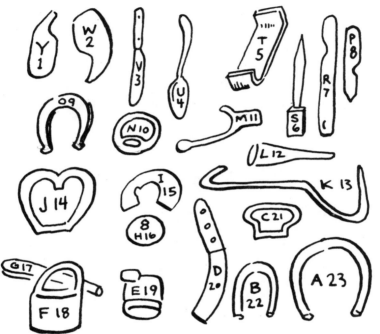

"__ __ __   __   __ __ __ __   __ __ __ __ __ __   __ __ __   __ __ __,   __ __   __ __ __ __ __
18 9 7   15   16 23 3 19   21 16 9 6 19 10   16 15 11   6 9   5 16 23 5

__ __   __ __ __   __ __ __ __ __ __ __ __   __ __ __   __ __ __ __ __ __ __ __ __
16 19   11 23 1   21 9 11 11 23 10 20   16 15 6   21 16 15 12 20 7 19 10

__ __ __   __ __ __   __ __ __ __ __ __ __ __ __ __   __ __ __ __ __   __ __ __   __ __
23 10 20   16 15 6   16 9 4 6 19 16 9 12 20   23 18 5 19 7   16 15 11   5 9

__ __ __ __   __ __ __   __ __ __   __ __   __ __ __ __   __ __ __ __   __ __
13 19 19 8   5 16 19   2 23 1   9 18   5 16 19   12 9 7 20   22 1

__ __ __ __ __   __ __ __ __ __ __ __ __ __ __ __ __   __ __ __
20 9 15 10 17   7 15 17 16 5 19 9 4 6 10 19 6 6   23 10 20

_ _ _ _ _ _ _ , _ _   _ _ _ _   _ _ _   _ _ _ _   _ _ _
14 4 6 5 15 21 19 6 9   5 16 23 5   5 16 19   12 9 7 20   11 23 1

_ _ _ _ _   _ _ _ _ _   _ _ _ _ _ _   _ _ _ _   _ _
22 7 15 10 17   4 8 9 10   23 22 7 23 16 23 11   2 16 23 5   16 19

_ _ _   _ _ _ _ _ _   _ _ _ _ _   _ _ _ ."
16 23 6   6 8 9 13 19 10   23 22 9 4 5   16 15 11

_ _ _ _ _ _ _ 18:19
17 19 10 19 6 15 6

Now as you practice saying your verse three times today, determine in your heart to be like Abraham. God has chosen you—so keep His ways by doing righteousness and justice, and God will bless you just like He did Abraham.

GOD REVEALS HIS PLAN TO ABRAHAM

As Max and Molly followed the wagon train, Max noticed a funny-looking rock formation off in the distance.

"Hey, Dad," Max shouted to be heard over the loud creaking of the wagons, "is that Chimney Rock over there in the distance?"

Max's dad hung his head out of the wagon to yell an answer back to Max. "It sure is, buddy. We'll be making camp in about 20 minutes at the base of Chimney Rock."

Max looked at Molly. "We're going to be camping in the exact same spot as many of the pioneers. Chimney Rock was one of their favorite camping spots along the way because it had a good water source. Isn't that cool?"

"It sure is. Hey, let's draw a picture of Chimney Rock when we make camp," Molly told Max, "just like the pioneer kids did on the trail."

So how are you holding up on the hot, dusty trail? I bet you're ready for some nice, cool water to drink. Why don't you dip your cup into the water barrel as we head back to Genesis 18?

Let's find out what God reveals to Abraham about what He is about to do. But don't forget to talk with your Wagon Master first before you continue your journey.

In Genesis 18:17-19 we saw the Lord say that He had chosen Abraham, and He would not hide from Abraham what He was about to do. Does God ever hide what He is up to from His children? Let's do some cross-referencing to find out.

Look up and read Amos 3:7.

Amos 3:7 To WHOM does God reveal His secret counsel?

_____

Now look up and read Revelation 1:1.

Revelation 1:1 WHAT did God reveal to His bond-servants?

The _____ which must soon _____ _____

Do you see how God never hides from us what He is about to do? We can know what God is going to do in the future, because we have His complete Word. We have the whole Bible.

Now let's head back to Genesis 18:20 on page 172.

Genesis 18:20 WHAT does the Lord say about Sodom and Gomorrah?

Their _____ is exceedingly_____.

Genesis 18:21 WHAT is the Lord going to do?

_____

Genesis 18:22,23 WHAT does Abraham ask the Lord after the two men have headed toward Sodom?

"Will You indeed _____ _____ the

_____ with the_____?"

Genesis 18:24,25 WHAT does Abraham say about the Lord?

"Shall not the _____ of all the _____

deal _____?"

Genesis 18:26 HOW does the Lord respond?

"If I find in Sodom _____ _____

within the city, then I will _____ the whole place

on their account."

Genesis 18:27 As Abraham speaks again to the Lord,
WHAT does he recognize about himself?

"I am but _____ and _____."

Now in Genesis 18:28-32 we see Abraham continuing to
ask the Lord WHAT He would do if there are different
numbers of righteous men:

Verse 28 _____ righteous men

Verse 29 _____ righteous men

Verse 30 _____ righteous men

Verse 31 _____ righteous men

Verse 32 _____ righteous men

WHAT does it mean to be righteous? Do you remember? To
be righteous is to be right with God. A righteous person is
someone who realizes that he is a sinner and has confessed
his sins so he now has a right relationship with God. He
wants to do what God says is right.

Genesis 18:32 WHAT does the Lord tell Abraham?

_____

Isn't it awesome to see how the Lord listened to Abraham's plea? Abraham asks the Lord if He will treat the wicked and the righteous the same way.

Abraham knows that the Lord is a fair God who judges justly. He pleads for the Lord to look and see if there are any righteous persons in Sodom and to spare the city for the sake of the righteous. WHAT happened? The Lord answered Abraham that He would spare the city if only ten righteous people are found.

We also have the awesome opportunity of having God hear our pleas. We can go to God in prayer and plead for God's help for our country, just like Abraham did for Sodom and Gomorrah. Will God hear us? Look up and read 1 John 5:14,15.

We can ask God anything if we ask HOW?

"If we ask anything _____ to His

_____, He _____ us. And if we know that

He _____ us in whatever we _____, we know

that we have the _____ which we have asked

from Him."

Have you prayed for your city and country? We live in a very wicked world that is a lot like Sodom and Gomorrah. We need to go to God in prayer and plead for the sake of our country.

We need to ask God to turn the people of our country's hearts back to Him—to help us truly have a country that is one nation under God, before He decides to bring judgment on us like He did on Sodom and Gomorrah.

Now HOW did Abraham ask? We see Abraham approach the Lord by telling Him that he is but dust and ashes. Abraham knew his place. He was speaking with a holy and righteous God.

HOW do you treat God? Do you treat Him as the holy God that He is?

Write out HOW you approach God.

_____

Now pray by bowing before a holy God, praising Him for who He is, and asking Him to turn the hearts of the people in your country back to Him!

TWO ANGELS IN SODOM

Murph pulled the wagon up next to the campsite and halted Sally and Chip. As he unhitched the horses, everyone stretched and laughed about the bumpy, creaking journey across the prairie.

Max's mom said, "Can you imagine riding in those wagons day after day for five months?"

"No way," replied Max's Aunt Sherry. "Now I know just how easy we have it."

"Well," Aunt Kathy laughed, "I guess it's time to become real pioneer women. Let's call the kids and go help Murph get dinner started."

As they approached Murph at the wagon, he was already unpacking the ingredients for tonight's dinner. "What's that?" Max asked, as Murph handed him a small shaker and asked him to shake it into a pot of beans, ham, and onions. "It's my own special seasoning called 'Romping Red.' It'll make these beans extra good so that even you will be asking for extra helpings."

"I don't think so, Murph," Max laughed. "But I'll try it, just to see."

As Max finished seasoning the beans, Murph carried them and placed them over an open campfire. "In a little while, sis," he told Molly, "I'll let you use my own special 'trail dust' seasoning as we flour and season our steak for our special campfire stew."

"Yum," Molly replied. "That sounds really good. Can we go check out Chimney Rock while we're waiting, Murph?"

"You sure can, sis," Murph answered, "but you have to stay on the side with the grass as you climb up to the top. The soft clay is really slick, and you don't want to slide down faster than you go up."

"We'll be careful," Max said. "Sam, come on, boy. Let's go climb another cool rock."

Now as you head across the prairie to climb Chimney Rock, let's pull out God's map so we can mark what's happening in Sodom and Gomorrah. Turn to page 173. Read Genesis 19 and mark the following key words:

Abraham (color it blue)

Lot (color it orange)

two angels (color it yellow)

destroy (draw black squiggly lines)

Don't forget to mark anything that tells you WHERE by double-underlining the <u>WHERE</u> in green. And don't forget to mark anything that tells you WHEN by drawing a green clock like this: 🕐

Practice saying your memory verse three times in a row, three times today! Now head back to the campfire and help Murph throw a little "trail dust" on that campfire stew.

ESCAPE FROM SODOM

"Mmmm, that was really good, Murph," Max said as he finished up the last of his campfire stew and beans.

"Glad you liked it," Murph replied. "Now, as soon as you and Molly clean those cups and plates, I'll teach you how to fire a black powder rifle."

"You mean it, Murph? You'll really let us fire a real black powder rifle like the pioneers?"

"I sure will," said Murph, "as long as it is okay with your parents. I'll also show you how so many pioneers were killed because they did not know how to use their rifles."

Molly and Max both hurried to wash their plates and help clean up the campsite so they could get their first lesson in using a rifle.

"First we have to pour some of this black powder in our barrel," Murph explained. "Then we take our wad and put it in our mouth to get it really wet."

"Yuck," Molly said as she watched Max take his wad out of his mouth. "That is really gross!"

"Next, you wrap your bullet in your wad and drop it down into the barrel. Then you use your rod to make sure that the bullet is pushed all the way down. That's one of the mistakes the pioneers made—not getting their bullet all the way down.

"Okay, now you need to pull back the hammer and place your firing cap. Great. Now find your target, aim, and squeeze the trigger, but be prepared. It's going to be loud, and it is going to kick."

As Max fired the rifle, Molly covered her ears. "Cool," Max said after he had shot the rifle. "It's your turn, Molly. Put your wad in your mouth and get ready to load."

Now that we've all had a chance to shoot the rifle, we need to head back to Genesis to find out what happens when the two angels arrive in Sodom and Gomorrah. Turn to page 173 and read Genesis 19.

Genesis 19:1 WHO do the two angels see sitting at the gate as they arrive in Sodom?

_____

Did you know that the town rulers were the ones who sat at the gate to give judgment? Sitting at the gate implied you had power and authority in that city.

Genesis 19:1 WHAT does Lot do as he sees these angels?

_____

Genesis 19:2 WHAT does Lot ask them to do?

_____

Genesis 19:2 WHAT was the angels' response?

_____

Genesis 19:3 Did Lot agree that they should spend the night in the square? WHAT did he urge them to do?

_____

Genesis 19:4,5 WHAT happened that night?

The _____ of the _____surrounded Lot's

_____ and called for Lot to bring the two angels

out so they could have _____ with them.

Genesis 19:6,7 WHAT did Lot say to them?

"Please, my _____, do not act

_____."

Genesis 19:9 WHAT did the men of the city try to do?

They _____ hard against Lot and came near to

_____ the _____.

Genesis 19:10 WHAT did the men (the angels) do?

They brought _____ into the house with them,

and _____ the door.

Genesis 19:11 WHAT did they do to the men at the doorway of the house?

_____

Genesis 19:12 WHAT did the angels tell Lot to do?

_____

Genesis 19:13 WHAT were the angels about to do?

_____

Genesis 19:16 WHAT did Lot do?

He _____.

Genesis 19:16 WHAT did the angels do?

_____

Genesis 19:16 WHY?

Because the _____ of the Lord was upon him.

Genesis 19:17 WHAT did they tell Lot and his family to do?

_____

_____

_____

Genesis 19:24 WHAT did God do?

_____

Genesis 19:26 WHAT did his wife do?

_____

Genesis 19:26 WHAT happened to her?

_____

Genesis 19:28 WHAT did Abraham see?

_____

Genesis 19:29 WHY did God send Lot out of the midst of the overthrow?

He _____ Abraham.

Genesis 19:30 WHERE did Lot go and stay with his two daughters?

_____

In Genesis 19:31-38 we see that Lot's two daughters were afraid that because of the utter destruction of the valley there would be no man left on earth to father their children. So WHAT did they do? Did they cry out to God for help, or did they take matters into their own hands?

Genesis 19:32 WHAT did they get their father to do?

_____

Genesis 19:32 WHAT were they trying to preserve?

_____

Did they do the right thing or the wrong thing?

_____

Genesis 19:37 WHAT did the first daughter of Lot name her son?

_____; he is the father of the_____

Genesis 19:38 WHAT did the younger daughter of Lot name her son?

_____; he is the father of the sons of_____

Isn't that amazing to see that the Lord rescued Lot because of Abraham? Did you notice in verse 16 how Lot hesitated? But because of the Lord's compassion, the angels seized his hand and brought him outside the city.

WHY did Lot hesitate? He knew Sodom was extremely wicked. He had just experienced their wickedness as they tried to break his door to take the angels. This just shows how sin can get us in a stronghold and we can't let go.

These men of the city were extremely wicked. They were committing acts of immorality that God tells us in His Word are wrong. Yet when Lot was warned that the city was about to be destroyed, he hesitated.

Have you ever hesitated when you saw your friends doing something wrong? Or did you walk away immediately? Write out what you did.

_____

Way to go! You have done an awesome job at following God's map. Now look at the drawing of Chimney Rock on page 95. What does it look like to you in the moonlight? Some people think it looks like a howling coyote. WHAT do you think? Speaking of coyotes, I hope we don't hear any as we crawl inside our tents. We need to get a good night's sleep because the pony express will be here early in the morning to pick up our mail!

A WICKED AND DESOLATE CITY

"I hear him, Uncle Jake," Max called as he headed toward the campsite. "I hear the pony express rider. He's on his way."

Molly ran outside her tent with her letter in her hand while Sam started running around, barking excitedly at all of the commotion going on around the wagons. Uncle Jake, Max, Molly, and Sam walked a little way up the ridge to see if they could see anything.

"Here he comes!" Max shouted from the ridge. "I see his red shirt. He is on the way!" Everyone gathered around the campfire as Murph worked on his special cowboy breakfast. They watched the pony express rider come into camp with a special letter addressed to Molly and Max.

"Look!" Molly exclaimed. "We got mail!"

As Max and Molly handed their mail to the pony express rider, he threw their letters inside his pouch and mounted his horse in a flash to continue on his journey of delivering the mail, just the way they did it in the pioneers' day.

Now that the excitement is over, Murph is ready for us to sit down and eat his famous cowboy breakfast. WHAT is a cowboy breakfast? It's everything that you have left over thrown into a huge cast iron skillet. Let's see, there's steak from our stew, onions, taters, cheese, eggs, bacon, and sausage. Watch out for Sam! He's standing right beside you on his hind legs sniffing your plate, and you know how he loves to snitch your bacon!

Now as we eat our breakfast, let's take another look at Sodom and Gomorrah. Did you know that Sodom is mentioned 48 times in 14 books of the Bible? WHY do you think God has written so much about Sodom?

Obviously there is something He wants to teach us. So let's pray. Then we need to take out God's map. We need to look up the references that are listed on the next page to find out what Sodom was like, how Lot got there, what the people were like in Sodom, and what Sodom is like today.

WHAT is Sodom like?

Genesis 13:10 In the valley of the _____

It was well _____.

WHAT were the people like in Sodom?

Genesis 13:13 The men of Sodom were _____

exceedingly and _____ against

the _____.

Jude 1:7 Sodom and Gomorrah and the cities around

them indulged in gross _____ and

went after strange flesh, and are exhibited as an

example in undergoing the _____

of eternal _____.

HOW does Lot get there?

Genesis 13:11 _____ chose to live in the valley of

the _____.

Genesis 13:12 _____ moved his tents as far as

_____.

Genesis 14:12 They took _____, for he was living in

Sodom.

WHAT did living in Sodom do to Lot?

2 Peter 2:6-8 He rescued _____ Lot, _____

by the sensual _____ of

_____ men, for by what he

_____ and _____, while living

among them, felt his _____ soul

_____ day after _____

by their _____ _____.

WHAT did God do to Sodom? WHAT is it like today?

Deuteronomy 29:23 All its land is _____ and

_____, a burning _____,

_____ and _____,

and no _____ grows in it. The Lord

overthrew it in His _____ and in His

_____.

Jeremiah 50:40 _____ overthrew Sodom and

Gomorrah with its _____. No man

will _____ there, nor will any son of man

_____ in it.

So let's look at what we discovered. Did you notice how in Genesis 13 Sodom was well watered and looked so good that Lot chose to live near there? Draw a picture of what Sodom looked like in Genesis 13:10 in the box on the next page.

Sodom in Genesis 13

As time goes by, we see that Lot goes from living near Sodom to living right inside the city. This shows us we can't stand on the outside of sin looking in because before we know it we are caught right in the middle. Remember what we saw in 2 Peter 2:6-8: Lot was a righteous man living in the middle of sin. He was tormented, being pulled in two different directions. For example, it's like hanging around with kids at school who use bad language. The next thing you know, you hear one of those words coming out of your mouth because you have exposed yourself to hearing it over and over again.

- Are you standing on the edge of sin by hanging around with kids who do things they shouldn't do, like using bad language, smoking, or drinking? ____Yes ____No

- WHAT are you going to do about it so that you don't end up right in the middle of sin, like Lot did?

_____

We also saw that the men in the city were exceedingly wicked and sinners against the Lord (Genesis 13:13). In Jude 1:7

we see that these people committed gross acts of immorality by using their bodies in a way that God says is sin.

God created male and female to be joined together to become one flesh inside a marriage relationship (Genesis 2:24), and any intimate physical relationship outside of a husband-and-wife relationship is sin.

The men of Sodom were dishonoring a relationship that God had created for a husband and a wife by having a physical relationship that was outside of marriage, and by being with other men, which God shows us in His Word is wrong. Look up and read Leviticus 18:22; 20:13; and Romans 1:18-32.

WHAT did we see happen to Sodom because of their wickedness and immorality? God utterly destroyed the city and all the cities around it. We saw that even today no man will ever live in it (Jeremiah 50:40), and that the land is unsown, unproductive, and no grass grows in it (Deuteronomy 29:23). Draw a picture of what Sodom looked like after God destroyed it in the box below.

Sodom

WHAT do you think God wants us to see? How about how He deals with wickedness and immorality? God uses Sodom as an example to show us how He deals with sin.

Look up and read 1 Corinthians 6:9-11.

1 Corinthians 6:9 WHO will not inherit the kingdom of God?

The _____

Now list those that God says are unrighteous in verses 9-10.

_____

_____

God has given us the example of Sodom and Gomorrah to show us what happens when we continue in our sin. God will bring judgment on those who are unrighteous, the wicked, unless they change their ways.

• Has God shown you anything in your life that is sin?

_____ Yes _____ No

• Are you willing to change it—to turn away from it and not do it anymore? _____ Yes _____ No

If so, then all you need to do is go to God and tell Him what you have done wrong, and that you want to be forgiven of that sin (1 John 1:9).

Now say your memory verse out loud to remind you that God has chosen you. So keep His ways by doing righteousness and justice.

Great work! It's time to load up those wagons and head back to the ranch so we can continue our trek across the Oregon Trail!

5

ABRAHAM CELEBRATES

GENESIS 20–21

Wasn't it awesome driving a real covered wagon across the prairie and camping out at Chimney Rock? Now you know what it feels like to be a real pioneer!

This week as we continue our journey, we will follow Abraham as he leaves the oaks of Mamre to journey toward the land of the Negev. We need to discover WHERE he settles and WHAT happens to him there.

ABRAHAM'S DECEPTION

"Hey, Dad," Max called as he and Molly looked out the window of the SUV. "Is that Scotts Bluff up ahead?"

"It sure is. Why don't we drive to the top this time instead of hiking and spend some time on the overlook trails? That way we will still have time to make it to Wyoming to see Fort Laramie, Register Cliff, and the Guernsey Ruts where there are still ruts up to five feet deep in some places today."

"That sounds like a great idea, but what is Register Cliff?" asked Molly.

Molly's mom answered, "Register Cliff was a popular campsite for the pioneers, and was about a day's travel from Fort Laramie. The pioneers who passed through here would carve their names in the sandstone cliff, registering that they had made it this far on the Oregon Trail."

"Hey, that's pretty cool," replied Max. "Can you still see their names today?"

"Yes, you can," replied Max's Aunt Kathy. "Although some of the signatures have eroded away, there are many that you can still see. You can also see some of the remnants of the trails, along with some of the unknown pioneers' graves."

"Now why don't you and Molly pull out God's map as we head up to the top of Scotts Bluff and find out what is happening with Abraham?"

"Great idea," Molly replied. "Let's pray."

Let's turn to page 177. Read Genesis 20 and mark the following key words:

God (draw a purple triangle and color it yellow)

Abraham (color it blue)

dream (draw a blue cloud)

nation (color it green and underline it in brown)

sin, sinned, sinning (color it brown)

pray, prayed (draw pray in purple and color it pink)

Don't forget to mark anything that tells you WHERE by double-underlining the WHERE in green. And don't forget to mark anything that tells you WHEN by drawing a green clock like this: 🕐

Now let's ask the 5 W's and an H.

Genesis 20:1 Look at Abraham's journey. WHERE did he stop to sojourn?

_____

Take a look at your map. Check out where Abraham stopped and circle the place in green.

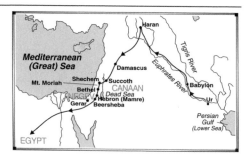

Genesis 20:2 WHAT does Abraham tell Abimelech, the king of Gerar, about Sarah?

_____

Genesis 20:2 WHAT does Abimelech do?

_____

Genesis 20:3 WHAT did God do?

_____

Genesis 20:3 WHAT did God say to Abimelech?

"You are a _____ _____ because of the

woman whom you have taken, for she is _____."

Genesis 20:4-5 Did Abimelech know that he had done the wrong thing when he took Sarah?

_____

Genesis 20:6 WHAT was God's reply?

"I know that in the _____ of your heart you

have done this. I also _____ you from _____

against Me. I did not let you _____ her."

Genesis 20:7 WHAT did God tell Abimelech to do?

_____

Genesis 20:7 WHAT did God say Abraham would do for Abimelech?

"He will _____ for you."

Genesis 20:9-10 WHAT did Abimelech ask Abraham?

_____

Genesis 20:11 WHAT is Abraham's answer?

_____

Genesis 20:14 WHAT did Abimelech give Abraham?

_____

Genesis 20:15 WHAT did Abimelech tell Abraham to do?

_____

Genesis 20:16 WHAT did Abimelech give Abraham as vindication for Sarah?

_____

Genesis 20:17 WHAT did Abraham do?

He _____ to God.

Genesis 20:17 WHAT did God do?

_____

Can you believe that Abraham made the same mistake that he made in Genesis 12? We see that even though Abraham is a righteous man, he still makes mistakes. Isn't it awesome to see that God loves and accepts us, even though we aren't perfect? Our relationship with God isn't based on our performance but on His love and mercy.

Did you notice how God steps in and intervenes by protecting Sarah from Abraham's mistake? God is always in control, even when we take matters into our own hands. Look at how God knew Abimelech's heart and kept him from sinning. God is a sovereign God. He protects His covenant. No one can thwart His plans!

All right! Now climb out of the SUV. We have arrived at Register Cliff. Aren't these cliffs awesome? Look! Someone has carved our memory verse on the cliff, but they carved it backwards.

You need to look at the first line of letters, starting on the far right, and write each letter from right to left on the first line below. Then you need to do the same thing for the next six lines of letters to unscramble this verse. Now look up Romans 4 in your Bible to discover the reference for these verses.

EHT OT TCEPSER HTIW TEY
REVAW TON DID EH DOG FO ESIMORP
NI GNORTS WERG TUB FEILEBNU NI
DNA DOG OT YROLG GNIVIG HTIAF
TAHW TAHT DERUSSA YLLUF GNIEB
SAW EH DESIMORP DAH DOG
MROFREP OT OSLA ELBA

—Romans 4: ____ , ____

Way to go! Now don't forget to practice saying this verse. How many times in a row? _____ And how many times today? _____

A SPECIAL CELEBRATION

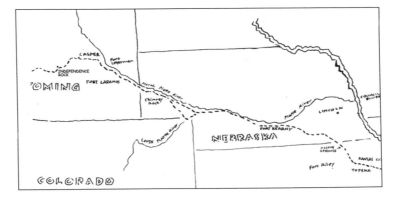

"I can't believe today is the Fourth of July, Independence Day," Max said as they headed down the road. "Do you think we'll get to shoot off some fireworks tonight?"

"Absolutely," replied Max's dad. "We're planning a picnic and a whole celebration, just like the pioneers did as they reached Independence Rock. The pioneers always camped and celebrated at Independence Rock, even if it wasn't the Fourth of July, because they knew they were almost halfway to Oregon when they arrived here. They also climbed to the top of Independence Rock and carved their names all over it, just like at Register Cliff."

"Are we almost there, Uncle Luke?" Molly asked.

"Yes," he replied. "Do you know what Independence Rock looks like?"

"Kind of like a huge turtle or a whale," Molly answered her Uncle Luke.

"That's right. So keep your eyes open. Let's see who can spot it first."

"That should be easy," laughed Molly's mom. "With all this barren land, a huge rock shaped like a turtle in the middle of nowhere shouldn't be too hard to spot."

Now as we keep our eyes open for Independence Rock, we need to head back to Genesis 21. It looks like Abraham and Sarah are also celebrating a special event. WHAT has happened since Abraham's encounter with King Abimelech? Let's find out. Read Genesis 21:1-21 beginning on page 178 and mark the following key words:

God (draw a purple triangle and color it yellow)

Abraham (color it blue)

nation (color it green and underline it in brown)

circumcised (draw a red knife)

Don't forget to mark anything that tells you WHERE by double-underlining the WHERE in green. And don't forget to mark anything that tells you WHEN by drawing a green clock like this: 🕐

Great work! Tomorrow we will continue to follow God's map as we take a closer look at Genesis 21.

ABRAHAM'S GREAT FEAST

"Wow! Just look at Independence Rock! It is so cool! Can we carry our picnic and eat on the top of the rock like some of the pioneers did?" asked Molly.

"That sounds like a really fun idea," answered Molly's Aunt Jena. "That is, if your mom and I can make it to the top with all the food intact."

"We'll help," Max volunteered, and Sam barked his agreement.

"Then let's get started," said Max's dad as he started unloading the food from the car.

All of a sudden there was a flash of white, brown, and black. Max looked surprised until he realized what had happened. Then he took off running, yelling "Sam, come back here!"

Now as Max tries to catch Sam so they can picnic on top of the rock, let's head back to Genesis 21 on page 178 and ask the 5W's and an H.

Genesis 21:1-3 WHAT has finally happened for Abraham and Sarah?

Sarah bore a _____ to Abraham, and Abraham

named him _____.

Genesis 21:4 WHAT did Abraham do when Isaac was eight days old?

He _____ his son as _____ had

commanded him.

Genesis 21:5 HOW old is Abraham?

_____ years old

HOW old is Sarah (remember, she is ten years younger than Abraham)?

_____ years old

Genesis 21:6 WHAT did Sarah say God has made for her?

_____

Genesis 21:8 WHAT did Abraham make to celebrate the day Isaac was weaned? A great _____

Genesis 21:9 WHAT did Sarah see Ishmael (Hagar's son) doing at the feast? He was _____ Isaac.

Genesis 21:10 WHAT did Sarah tell Abraham to do?

"_____ _____ this maid and her son."

(Circle these two words together in the word search on page 120.)

WHY? Because "the son of this maid shall not be an

_____ with my son Isaac."

Genesis 21:11 HOW did Abraham feel about driving out Ishmael?

He was _____.

Genesis 21:12-13 WHAT did God tell Abraham to do?

_____ to Sarah because it is through Isaac

your descendants will be named.

Genesis 21:13 WHAT did God say about the son of the
maid?

"And the son of the maid I will make a _____

also, because he is your descendant."

Genesis 21:14 WHAT did Abraham do?

He rose early in the morning and took _____

and a skin of _____ and gave them to

_____, and gave her the _____, and

_____ her away.

Genesis 21:14 WHERE did Hagar wander?

In the _____ of Beersheba

Genesis 21:16 WHAT did Hagar do?

She lifted up her voice and _____.

Genesis 21:17 WHO heard the lad (Ishmael) crying?

_____

Genesis 21:17 WHAT did the angel tell Hagar?

"Do not _____, for God has _____ the

voice of the lad where he is."

Genesis 21:18,19 WHAT did God open her eyes to see?

A well of _____

Genesis 21:20,21 WHAT happened to Ishmael?

God was with him, he _____, lived in the wilderness,

and became an _____. His mother took a

_____ for him from the land of _____.

Now find the answer from each blank and circle it in the word search below. Remember, if a word is used more than once, you only have to find and circle it one time.

D	I	S	T	R	E	S	S	E	D	D	S
E	T	U	O	E	V	I	R	D	E	L	S
S	G	N	I	K	C	O	M	R	L	A	E
I	B	O	H	E	A	R	D	E	I	U	N
C	R	I	Y	O	B	N	Y	H	S	G	R
M	E	T	Y	S	U	T	W	C	T	H	E
U	A	A	E	H	E	I	R	R	E	T	D
C	D	N	E	N	F	D	E	A	N	E	L
R	T	N	I	E	G	Y	P	T	G	R	I
I	O	N	A	C	A	A	S	I	V	A	W
C	O	S	W	A	T	E	R	A	E	F	H
S	T	G	R	E	W	E	P	T	G	O	D

Wow! Finally after all these years, Abraham and Sarah have been given their son! God has fulfilled His covenant promise

in His timing and in His way. Have you ever had to wait for God to answer your prayer? After God answered, did you see how His timing and His way was so much better than you could have imagined? Remember, God's ways are always best, even if it is a long, hard wait!

Now are you ready to shoot off some fireworks with Max, Molly, and Sam? Light up God's magnificent creation as you practice your memory verse.

ABRAHAM'S FAiTH

"We're on the road again," Max and Molly both sang as they left Independence Rock, heading down the highway with Sam licking Max's face, trying to get him to stop singing.

Molly laughed. "I don't think Sam wants us to sing anymore. Hey, Uncle Luke, why are we pulling off so soon?"

"Devil's Gate is down this road. I thought you might want to have a quick look before we head on to Fort Bridger."

"What is Devil's Gate, Dad?" asked Max.

"It's a rough-looking chasm carved through solid granite by the Sweetwater River. The pioneers' wagons couldn't go through the gap, so they had to pass it to the south. But a lot of them hiked over, just so they could get a closer look."

"Hey, that's pretty neat," Molly said as they climbed out and hiked down the path.

Now that we have seen Devil's Gate and are back on the road once again, let's pull out God's map to find out how Abraham and Sarah could have had a son at such an old age.

Don't forget to talk to your Wagon Master, then read Hebrews 11:11,12 on page 193.

Now turn to page 197 and read Romans 4:13-25. Let's mark the following key words:

God (draw a purple triangle and color it yellow)

Jesus (draw a purple cross and color it yellow)

Abraham (color it blue)

Sarah (color it pink)

faith (believe) (draw a purple book and color it green)

credited (color it orange)

promise (circle it in red)

grace (draw a yellow box and color it blue)

Law (draw black tablets)

All right! Now, let's make a list below of what we have learned from both Hebrews and Romans about Abraham, Sarah, God, and Jesus Christ.

Abraham

Hebrews 11:12 He was as good as _____ when

he had Isaac. (This means his body was past the

ability to father children.)

His descendants were as many as the _____ of

heaven in number and innumerable as the

_____ which is by the seashore.

Romans 4:13 The _____ to Abraham was not

through the _____, but through the

righteousness of _____.

Romans 4:16 It is by f __ __ __ h with g __ __ __ __ that

the _____ may be guaranteed to all the

descendants, not just the ones of the Law, but to

those who are of the f __ __ __ h of Abraham,

the _____ of us all.

Romans 4:17,18 In hope against hope he _____ God.

Romans 4:19 He did not become _____ in faith.

He was about _____ years old.

Romans 4:20 He did not waver in _____ but

grew _____ in faith, giving

_____ to God.

Romans 4:22 It was credited to him as_____.

Sarah

Hebrews 11:11 By _____ Sarah received the ability

to _____, even beyond the

_____ time of _____ , since she

considered Him _____ who had

_____.

Romans 4:19 Her womb was d __ __ d.

God

Hebrews 11:11 God is f __ __ __ __ __ __ l.

God p __ __ __ __ __ __ d.

Romans 4:17 God made Abraham the father of

_____ _____ .

God gives _____ to the dead and calls into

_____ that which does not _____ .

Romans 4:21 God is able to p __ __ __ __ __ m what

He has promised.

Romans 4:24 God raised _____ our Lord from

the _____ .

Jesus Christ

Romans 4:24 Jesus was r __ __ __ __ d from the

_____ .

Romans 4:25 Jesus was _____ over because

of our _____ , and was raised

because of our _____ .

Isn't it amazing to see that it didn't matter that Abraham and Sarah were too old to have children because nothing is impossible with God? Don't you just love those verses in Romans 4:18-21 where it says in hope against hope he believed, that he did not waver in unbelief but grew strong in faith, giving

glory to God, being fully assured that what God had promised He was also able to perform? What awesome faith! No wonder Abraham is called God's friend!

WHAT did you learn about Jesus? Look at how He was delivered up to rescue us from our sin so we could be made right with God. What a lesson of blessings!

Why don't you take just a moment to thank God for being faithful and for always keeping His promises!

CUTTING COVENANT

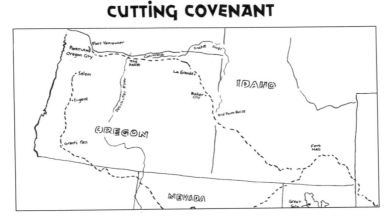

"Hey, guys," Molly's dad said as the SUV pulled into Hooper Spring in Soda Springs, Idaho. "We're here! Are you ready to try out the bubbling mineral water?"

"Sure! I'll race you, Molly!" Max said as he jumped out of the SUV and headed to the spring of water. "This is so cool. Look at all those bubbles."

"Here, Max," said Max's mom as she handed him his enamelware cup. "Dip your cup into the water and try some."

"Yuck!" Max said as he took a sip and squinched up his face. "This stuff is awful! Did the pioneers really like drinking this stuff?"

"Let me try," Molly said, taking a careful sip from Max's cup. "Ohhh, that is really weird-tasting. What's in this water?"

"Oh, silica, iron, calcium, magnesium, and bicarbonate radicle," laughed her mom. "Lots of good stuff."

"I don't think so," Max said. "Hey, let's see if Sam will drink it. He'll try anything." Max held Sam while Molly tried to get him to lick the water out of the cup. Sam just sniffed it and turned away. "Come on, Sam," Max laughed, "you'll like it. I know you will."

Everyone laughed as Sam jumped out of Max's arms and started sniffing around the spring. "I think we have finally found something even Sam won't try," said Max's dad.

While we take a break here by the springs, let's pull out God's map and finish reading and marking the key words for Genesis 21.

Have you prayed, brave explorers? Then turn to pages 180-181. Read Genesis 21:22-34 and mark the following key words:

God (draw a purple triangle and color it yellow)

Abraham (color it blue)

covenant (draw a yellow box and color it red)

Don't forget to mark anything that tells you WHERE by double-underlining the WHERE in green. And don't forget to mark anything that tells you WHEN by drawing a green clock like this:

Genesis 21:22 WHO spoke to Abraham?

_____ and _____, the commander

of his army

Genesis 21:22 WHAT do they say to Abraham?

"_____ is with you in _____ that you do."

Isn't that an awesome testimony?

Genesis 21:23 WHAT does Abimelech want?

For Abraham to _____ by God that he will not

deal _____ with him, or with his

_____, or with his _____—to

show him the same _____ that he has shown

to Abraham as he has sojourned in his land.

Genesis 21:24 WHAT does Abraham say?

_____

Genesis 21:25 WHAT is Abraham's complaint?

_____

Genesis 21:26 Did Abimelech know about this problem?

_____

Genesis 21:27 WHAT did Abraham give Abimelech?

_____

Genesis 21:27 WHAT did they make?

_____

Genesis 21:28 WHAT does Abraham do?

_____

Genesis 21:30 WHAT did this mean?

_____

Genesis 21:31 WHY is this place called Beersheba?

_____

Genesis 21:32 WHAT happened after they made their covenant?

_____

Genesis 21:33 WHAT did Abraham do?

He _____ a _____ tree at Beersheba,

and he called on the _____ of the

_____, the _____ God.

Genesis 21:34 HOW long did Abraham stay in the land of the Philistines?

_____

Did you notice that after Abraham cut a covenant with Abimelech, he plants a tamarisk tree and calls on the name of the Lord? This is the first use of the name *El Olam,* showing God as the Everlasting God. Isn't that awesome to watch as Abraham continues to discover God's character and ways?

Why don't you spend a few minutes thinking about what you have seen about God?

Now as we sit by the geyser and wait for it to erupt, say your memory verse out loud to a grown-up! We are so proud of you!

6

ABRAHAM'S TEST OF FAITH

GENESIS 22–25:18

As we have trekked across the country following the pioneers' journey on the Oregon Trail, we have seen many of the hardships and trials that they faced along the way.

This week as we continue to follow Abraham in his journey of faith, we will see him face the greatest trial in his life as God tests His brave explorer's faith. Does Abraham truly fear God? Will he trust and obey?

GOD TESTS ABRAHAM

"Look," Max called out, as he spotted the huge swimming complex with a ten-foot-high diving platform. "Let's go there. It looks awesome!"

Max's mom smiled, "Guess what? We are—right after we visit the hot springs."

"What are hot springs?" asked Molly.

"The hot springs are pools of warm water that come bubbling up from a volcano. These springs are filled with

129

minerals, like the water you tasted at Soda Springs. But the water from these springs is very warm. The water temperature is from 102 to 104 degrees Fahrenheit. It's kind of like a natural hot tub where you can put on your swimsuit and soak in these bubbling mineral waters."

"That sounds neat," Molly replied. "But I'm with Max. That swimming pool place looks awesome. Did you see all of those water slides?"

"I did," replied Molly's mom. "Did you also see those kids tubing down the river? When we finish soaking at the hot springs, we're going to hop into some of those tubes and float down the river to the swimming pool complex."

"Really?" Max almost shouted. "All right! Sam, you are in for the adventure of your life."

Max's mom laughed. "I don't know if I can handle Sam floating down the river in a tube, but we'll give it a try. We'll head for the springs right after our picnic."

Now let's find out what is happening with Abraham after he makes a covenant with Abimelech and calls on God's name.

Okay, brave explorers, are you ready to continue your journey?

Then let's pray and turn to page 181. Read Genesis 22 and mark the following key words:

Abraham (color it blue)

tested (underline it in orange)

love (draw a red heart)

provide (circle it in blue and color it green)

worship (circle it in purple and color it blue)

obeyed (circle it in orange and color it yellow)

bless (draw a blue cloud and color it pink)

nations (color it green and underline it in brown)

Don't forget to mark anything that tells you WHERE by double-underlining the WHERE in green. And don't forget to mark anything that tells you WHEN by drawing a green clock like this: 🕐

Now let's find out what happened.

Genesis 22:1 WHAT did God do after these things?

God _____ Abraham.

Genesis 22:1 WHAT was Abraham's response to God's call?

_____

Genesis 22:2 WHAT did God tell Abraham to do?

"_____ now your _____, your _____

son, whom you _____, _____, and go to the

land of _____, and _____ him there as

a _____ _____ on one of the mountains

of which I will tell you."

Look up and read John 3:16. WHO was God's only begotten Son?

_____

Genesis 22:3 HOW did Abraham respond? WHAT did he do?

_____

_____

Genesis 22:4 HOW many days did it take Abraham to get there?

_____

Genesis 22:5 WHAT did Abraham tell his young men?

"_____ here with the donkey, and I and the

_____ will go over there; and we will

_____ and _____ to you."

Genesis 22:6 WHAT did Abraham lay on Isaac?

_____

Look up and read John 19:17. WHAT did Jesus carry?

His own _____

Genesis 22:6-7 WHAT was Isaac's question to Abraham?

_____

_____

Genesis 22:8 WHAT was Abraham's response?

"_____ will _____ for Himself the

_____ for the burnt offering."

Genesis 22:9-10 WHAT did Abraham do?

_____

_____

Genesis 22:11-12 WHAT did the angel of the Lord call out to Abraham?

"Do not _____ out your _____ against

the lad, and do nothing to _____; for now I know

that you _____ _____, since you have not

_____ your _____, your _____ son,

from _____."

Genesis 22:13 WHAT did Abraham see?

_____

WHAT did he do with this ram?

_____

Look up and read John 3:16 again. WHAT did God give as a sacrifice for our sins?

_____

Look up and read John 1:29. WHAT is Jesus?

The _____ of God

Genesis 22:14 WHAT did Abraham name that place?

_____

Genesis 22:15-17 WHAT did the angel of the Lord tell Abraham that the Lord was going to do because Abraham had not withheld his only son?

"I will greatly _____ you, and I will greatly

_____ your _____ as the _____ of

the heavens and as the _____ which is on the

seashore; and your _____ shall possess the

_____ of their enemies. "

Genesis 22:18 WHY would all the nations of the earth be blessed?

_____

Genesis 22:19 WHERE did Abraham live?

_____

Wow! What obedience! What incredible faith! After waiting 25 years for God to give him this child of the promise, God tells Abraham to sacrifice this only son that he loved.

Did you notice how he obeyed God immediately? There was no resistance. He didn't argue. He didn't ask why. He just got up the next morning and obeyed. God uses the word *love* here for the first time in the Bible to show a father offering up his only son.

Does this remind you of another Father who offered up His only Son? Did you notice how Abraham offering up his only son is a picture of what God did for us? Isaac was Abraham's only begotten son, the son of the promise, and Jesus was God's only begotten Son. Isaac carried his own wood for the sacrifice, just like Jesus carried the cross that He was sacrificed on. God provided a ram to take Isaac's place, while Jesus was the Lamb that was sacrificed in our place to pay for our sins. Isn't that awesome?

God tested Abraham. But what does Abraham call it? Look at Genesis 22:5. WHAT does Abraham say he and the lad will do? Worship. Do you know what worship is? Worship means to bow before God. It is to lie flat out before God because you recognize He is God and He is to be respected. It is to acknowledge God's worth, to honor God as God.

Abraham worshiped God. He held nothing back. He simply trusted and obeyed.

HOW about you?

- Does the way that you live show that God is first? Is there anything that you are holding onto instead of handing it over to God? Have you put something else in God's rightful place?

To truly worship God is to be willing to say, "I love You. I will trust You. I will honor and respect You. I will obey You and do what You tell me to do."

Think about your relationship with God and spend some time today with God in prayer.

Now as we go tubing down the river, you need to discover your memory verse. Take a look at the picture of the tubes below. Find the missing words from the tubes that fit into the blanks to complete your memory verse.

And the __ __ __ __ __ __ __ __ __ __ was

__ __ __ __ __ __ __ __ __ which says, "And

__ __ __ __ __ __ __ __ __ __ __ __ __ __

God, and it was __ __ __ __ __ __ __ to him as

__ __ __ __ __ __ __ __ __ __ __ __ ," and he

was called the __ __ __ __ __ __ of God.

—James 2:____

GOD'S HALL OF FAITH

"We had a great time yesterday, Dad," Max said. "Thanks."

"You're welcome," his dad replied with a smile on his face.

"Why are you smiling?" Max asked.

"Oh, I was just remembering Sam as he went spinning around in that tube when that little boy bumped into you, and you two got separated."

Molly started giggling. "Yeah, Sam started barking, then he hopped right into the river trying to dog-paddle against the current. That was so funny."

"Can you imagine what Sam would have been like at the Three Island Crossing with the pioneers?" asked Kyle, Molly's dad.

"He would probably have jumped off the wagon into the river and stirred up the horses," Luke replied. "That was a pretty rough crossing for the pioneers with all those swift currents."

"Is that where we're headed today, Dad?" asked Max.

"Yes, it is. In fact, we're going to be there as they reenact the crossing the pioneers made."

"Yeah!" Molly and Max both exclaimed. "We can't wait!"

Now as you head to Three Island Crossing, our last stop in Idaho, let's pull out God's map. We need to look at a cross-reference in Hebrews to find out what God has to say about Abraham in this great "hall of faith."

Turn to page 193. Read Hebrews 11:8-19 and mark the following key words:

God (draw a purple triangle and color it yellow)

Abraham (color it blue)

Sarah (color it pink)

faith, believe (draw a purple book and color it green)

obeyed (circle it in orange and color it yellow)

promise (circle in red)

tested (underline it in orange)

Now solve the crossword puzzle.

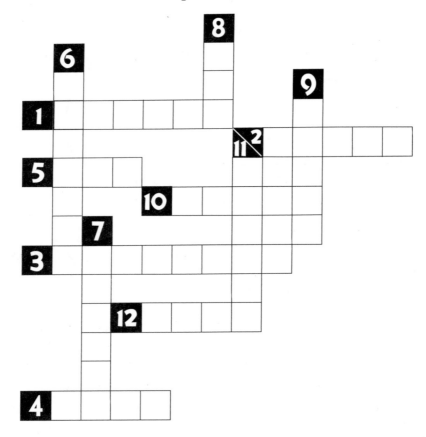

Hebrews 11:8 WHAT did Abraham do when he was called?

1. (Across) He _____.

Hebrews 11:17 HOW did Abraham offer up Isaac when he was tested?

2. (Across) By _____

Hebrews 11:17 WHAT had he received?

3. (Across) The _____

Hebrews 11:17 WHAT was he offering up?

4. (Across) His _____ begotten   5. (Across) _____

Now take a look back at Genesis 22:5. WHAT did Abraham say to his young men? "Stay here with the donkey, and I and the lad will go over there; and we will

6. (Down) _____ and

7. (Down) _____ to you."

This verse shows us that Abraham knew that Isaac was the son of the promise. Abraham would obey God by sacrificing his son, but he knew that he and Isaac would both return. HOW did he know this?

Go back to Hebrews 11:19. WHAT did Abraham consider?

8. (Down) That _____ is able to

9. (Down) _____ people even from the dead.

Now look up and read James 2:20-26 to finish your crossword puzzle.

James 2:22 HOW was faith perfected?

10. (Across) As a result of the _____

(That means that when we have faith, it will show by what we do.)

James 2:23 WHAT was Abraham called?

11. (Down) The _____ of God

James 2:26 WHAT is faith without works?

12. (Across) _____

Do you see how this passage in James fits what happened in Genesis 22:12? Abraham's works, his willingness to stretch out his hand to sacrifice his only son, showed his faith in God. Abraham knew God stands by His promises, and if he put Isaac to death, then God would have to raise him from the dead because the covenant promise was through Isaac. He was the child of the promise. Isn't that awesome faith?

HOW about you? Can other people see your faith by the way that you live and the things that you do?

That's why Abraham was called God's friend. Do you want to be a friend of God? Then walk like Abraham. Trust and obey. Let your faith be seen by your works.

JEHOVAH JIREH

As the SUV pulled into the park at Farewell Bend in Oregon, Max and Molly started cheering. Sam, not wanting to be left out of the action, barked and jumped around from seat to seat.

"Sam!" Luke said as Sam tried to jump onto his lap and help drive the SUV. "Get down, boy, before you make me have a wreck. We're here, everybody. Our first stop in the state of Oregon, Farewell Bend."

"Why is it called Farewell Bend, Dad?" asked Max.

"Because this is where the pioneers would tell the Snake River farewell as they started their trek across Oregon."

"It's really beautiful," Max's mom said. "Okay, everyone, let's get out and set up our camp. Then we can spend some time with God thanking Him for providing us with a safe trip.

"Just look at those mountains. God is an awesome Creator! Have you noticed how special all of His creation is as we have traveled across the different parts of the country?" Max's dad said.

Now while we sit by the river, spray some of that bug spray on. The mosquitoes are biting. Then let's head back to Genesis.

Turn to page 181. Read Genesis 22. Now look on your Observation Worksheet where you marked the key word *provide*. Make a list of all that you see about this word.

Provide

Genesis 22:8 _____ will provide for Himself the

_____ for the _____ _____.

Genesis 22:14 Abraham called the name of that place

The _____ _____ _____, as it is

said to this day, "In the _____ of the

_____ it will be _____."

Now draw a picture of this act of provision. Show Isaac on the altar while Abraham spots the ram in the thicket that God provided to take his son's place.

The Lord Will Provide

The Hebrew name for "the Lord Will Provide" is *Jehovah Jireh*. Isn't it awesome to know that God is our Provider? "In the mount of the Lord it will be provided." God provided a ram for Abraham to sacrifice in the place of Isaac.

Let's find out WHAT God has provided for you and me. Look up and read John 3:16-17.

John 3:16 WHOM did God provide as a sacrifice?

_____

WHY did God provide this sacrifice?

_____

If we believe in Jesus, WHAT will we have?

_____

John 3:17 WHY did God send Jesus into the world?

_____

Now look up and read John 1:29.

John 1:29 WHAT did John say when he saw Jesus coming to him?

"Behold, the _____ of _____ who takes

away the _____ of the world!"

Do you see just how much God loves you? He willingly gave up His only begotten Son to die in your place so that you would not perish—live in the lake of fire prepared for the devil and his angels forever. God provided Jesus, the Lamb of God, to die in our place to pay for our sins. God provided a way of escape for you and me.

Draw a picture of God's provision for us below.

God Provides a Lamb

Did you know that a burnt offering was a voluntary offering? It was an offering that was made in love as an act of worship. It's the offering that Noah offered God after the flood to worship Him (Genesis 8:20).

In Genesis 22:13 we see Abraham offering Isaac as a burnt offering.

Now let's use God's map to look up and read Leviticus 1 to find out about the burnt offering.

Leviticus 1:4 WHAT was the burnt offering for?

A _ _ _ _ _ _ _ _ t (a covering for sin)

Isn't that awesome to see that just as a burnt offering is done voluntarily for atonement, Jesus willingly laid His life on the altar to be sacrificed and make atonement for you and me?

Why don't you take some time to worship God, your Jehovah Jireh, thanking Him for the great price He paid for your sins because He loves you! Praise Him for providing all your needs.

Fantastic! Your journey is almost complete!

SARAH

"Mom, where did the pioneers head after Farewell Bend?" Max asked.

"Let's see, after Farewell Bend they had to travel through Burnt River Canyon, which was a huge obstacle," she replied.

"What kind of obstacle, Aunt Jena?" asked Molly.

"The canyon was very twisted, and even though it wasn't as bad as some of the other places on the trail, it sometimes took the wagon trains six days just to climb out of the canyon. By this time food was really scarce for the pioneers and their livestock."

"I bet they were tired of their long journey," Molly added.

"Yes, they were dirty, tired, starved, and some were broken-hearted after losing friends and family on the trail. They were very ready to reach Oregon City," replied Max's mom.

"I wonder if Abraham ever got tired of moving around?" Molly asked.

"I'm sure he did," replied her mom. "But Abraham was faithful to go wherever God led him. Why don't we pull out

God's map and read Genesis 23 to find out WHERE Abraham is and what is happening?"

Turn to page 183. Read Genesis 23 and mark the following key words:

Abraham (color it blue)

Sarah (color it pink)

Don't forget to mark anything that tells you WHERE by double-underlining the <u>WHERE</u> in green. And don't forget to mark anything that tells you WHEN by drawing a green clock like this: 🕐

Genesis 23:1-2 WHAT happens to Sarah?

_____

Genesis 23:1 HOW old was she?

_____

Genesis 23:2 WHERE did she die?

_____

WHAT did Abraham do?

_____

Genesis 23:7-9 WHAT did Abraham want to buy?

_____

Genesis 23:19 WHERE did Abraham bury Sarah?

_____

God's brave explorer has just lost his wife, like many people did on the Oregon Trail. Now let's look up 1 Peter 3:1-6 to find out what we can learn from Sarah's example. These are good things to remember because someday you may be a wife or have a wife of your own.

1 Peter 3:1 WHAT are wives to be to their husbands?

_____

WHY?

_____

1 Peter 3:2 WHAT kind of behavior is a wife to have?

_____

1 Peter 3:4 WHAT is precious in the sight of God?

_____

1 Peter 3:5,6 Is Sarah a good example?

_____

1 Peter 3:6 WHAT did Sarah do?

_____

Way to go! You are almost at the end of the trail. Now don't forget to practice your memory verse!

ABRAHAM, GOD'S FRIEND

"Look, we're here!" Molly yelled. "We did it! We are in Oregon City. We made it to the end of the trail!"

"I'll race you!" yelled Max as he headed toward the "End of the Oregon Trail" sign that was next to a 50-foot-high covered wagon museum building.

"I made it to the end of the trail first," laughed Max. "Let's go inside."

As their guide led them through a visual presentation, she passed around a fake buffalo chip to touch. "I am not touching that!" Molly stated, just as Max slapped it into the palm of her hand.

"Too late," he laughed. "You have to experience all of the Oregon Trail."

"Yuck, Max! I'm so glad I'm not a pioneer. I would not like gathering these all across the country." They all laughed as they finished up their tour and headed out to get some ice cream to celebrate the end of the trail.

Now as you lick that ice cream, let's finish our journey with Abraham. Let's head to Genesis 25. (We're going to skip Genesis 24 since it is all about Isaac. We'll learn about him in our next adventure.)

Let's find out what happens after Sarah dies. Turn to page 191 and read Genesis 25:1-18. Mark the following key words:

God (draw a purple triangle and color it yellow)

Abraham (color it blue)

blessed (draw a blue cloud and color it pink)

Don't forget to mark anything that tells you WHERE by double-underlining the <u><u>WHERE</u></u> in green. And don't forget to mark anything that tells you WHEN by drawing a green clock like this:

Genesis 25:1 WHAT does Abraham do?

_____

WHAT is her name?

_____

Genesis 25:2 WHO are her children?

_____

Genesis 25:5 WHO did Abraham give all that he had?

_____

Do you know why? Because God's promise of the inheritance was through Isaac, the child of the promise.

Genesis 25:6 WHAT did Abraham do for the other sons while he was still living?

_____

WHERE did Abraham send these other sons?

_____

Genesis 25:7 HOW old was Abraham?

_____

Genesis 25:8 WHAT happens to Abraham?

_____

Have you heard this before? Remember God's prophecy regarding Abraham's life in Genesis 15:15.

Genesis 25:8 WHAT do we see about Abraham?

He was _____ with life.

Genesis 25:9-10 WHERE did Isaac and Ishmael bury him?

_____

Genesis 25:11 WHAT did God do after Abraham died?

_____

Genesis 25:16 WHAT do we see about Ishmael's sons?

These sons are _____ _____ according to their tribes.

Did God prophesy he would have 12 princes?

_____

Genesis 25:17 HOW old is Ishmael when he dies?

_____

Genesis 25:18 WHAT do we see about Ishmael?

He settled in _____ of all his relatives.

Do you remember the prophecy given to Hagar about

Ishmael in Genesis 16:11-12? Did it come true?_____

Go back to Abraham's family tree on page 13 and add Abraham's new wife and their six sons.
Now let's take a last look at how Abraham is remembered by his descendants. Look up and read 2 Chronicles 20:7.

WHAT does Jehoshaphat call Abraham?

_____

Look up and read Isaiah 41:8.

WHAT does God call Abraham?

_____

Now look up and read James 2:23, your memory verse this week.

WHY was Abraham called God's friend?

_____

HOW will you be remembered? Will it be as God's friend?

Look up and read John 15:13-16.

John 15:14 HOW are you Jesus' friend?

_____

Abraham believed God's promises, and even though Abraham wasn't a perfect man, he was reckoned (declared) righteous by God because of his faith. He lived a life of obedience and faith. He was God's friend.

THE END OF THE TRAIL

All right! You did it! You made it to the end of the trail! What an awesome journey, as we camped our way across the United States. Just look at all we discovered about God's brave explorer—Abraham. What a man of faith and obedience!

As we followed God's brave explorer, we saw him make some very big mistakes, but he moved on. He returned to the Lord to call on His name, to worship, and to continue his journey of faith.

Wasn't it awesome to see our brave explorer believe God's promises and have it reckoned to him as righteousness? We saw Abraham get saved.

Just look at all we learned about God as we discovered that everything God does is based on covenant. God always keeps His promises. He is an awesome God! God is El Elyon—He is sovereign; He is in control over all of our circumstances. God is El Roi—He sees. We cannot run away or hide from Him.

God is El Shaddai—God Almighty. He is the powerful One, He is all-sufficient, and nothing is too difficult for Him! God is El Olam—the Everlasting God, and God is Jehovah Jireh—our Provider. He has provided salvation for you and me.

As we came to the end of the trail, we watched as God tested Abraham's faith. Abraham did not withhold anything from God—not even his only beloved son whom God had promised. Wasn't it amazing to discover that God loved us enough to sacrifice His Son so that we might have eternal life? Have you accepted this gift of salvation? Are you a child of the promise? Are you God's friend? Do you trust and obey?

As you continue your journey of faith, keep studying God's Word. We are so proud of you for doing these Bible studies!

Don't forget to fill out the card in the back of the book. We want to send you a special certificate for helping us search out truth as we followed God's brave explorer on his journey of faith.

Now on the way home we can do a little windsurfing in The Dalles or climb to the top of Multnomah Falls. It has been an incredible journey! See you for another adventure in God's Word real soon!

Molly, Max, and

(Sam)

PUZZLE ANSWERS

Pages 14-15

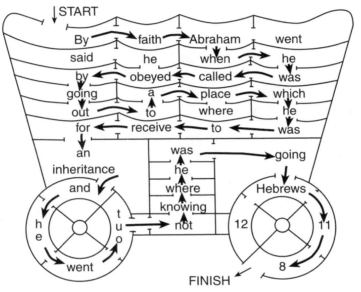

By faith Abraham, when he was called, obeyed by going out to a place which he was to receive for an inheritance; and he went out, not knowing where he was going.

—Hebrews 11:8

Page 45

Then he believed in the LORD; and He reckoned it to him as righteousness.

—Genesis 15:6

Page 52

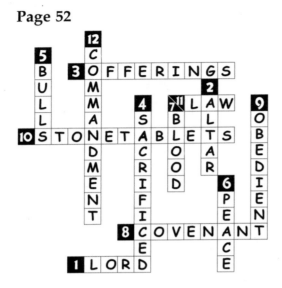

Page 69

... the Lord appeared to Abram and said to him, "I am God Almighty; walk before Me, and be blameless.

—Genesis 17:1

Page 80

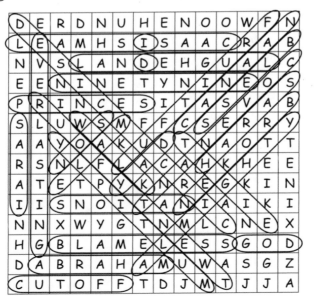

Pages 89-90

"FOR I HAVE CHOSEN HIM, SO THAT
18 9 7   15   16 23 3 19   21 16 9 6 19 10   16 15 11   6 9   5 16 23 5

HE MAY COMMAND HIS CHILDREN
16 19   11 23 1   21 9 11 11 23 10 20   16 15 6   21 16 15 12 20 7 19 10

AND HIS HOUSEHOLD AFTER HIM TO
23 10 20   16 15 6   16 9 4 6 19 16 9 12 20   23 18 5 19 7   16 15 11   5 9

KEEP THE WAY OF THE LORD BY
13 19 19 8   5 16 19   2 23 1   9 18   5 16 19   12 9 7 20   22 1

DOING RIGHTEOUSNESS AND
20 9 15 10 17   7 15 17 16 5 19 9 4 6 10 19 6 6   23 10 20

JUSTICE, SO THAT THE LORD MAY
14 4 6 5 15 21 19   6 9   5 16 23 5   5 16 19   12 9 7 20   11 23 1

BRING UPON ABRAHAM WHAT HE
22 7 15 10 17   4 8 9 10   23 22 7 23 16 23 11   2 16 23 5   16 19

HAS SPOKEN ABOUT HIM."
16 23 6   6 8 9 13 19 10   23 22 9 4 5   16 15 11

—GENESIS 18:19
17 19 10 19 6 15 6

Page 114

Yet, with respect to the promise of God, he did not waver in unbelief but grew strong in faith, giving glory to God, and being fully assured that what God had promised, He was able also to perform.

—Romans 4:20,21

Page 120

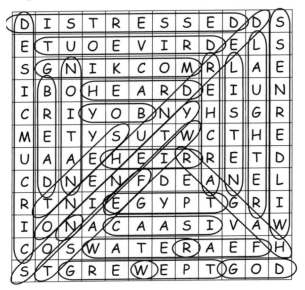

Page 136

And the <u>Scripture</u> was <u>fulfilled</u> which says, "And <u>Abraham</u> <u>believed</u> God, and it was <u>reckoned</u> to him as <u>righteousness</u>," and he was called the <u>friend</u> of God.

—James 2:23

Page 138

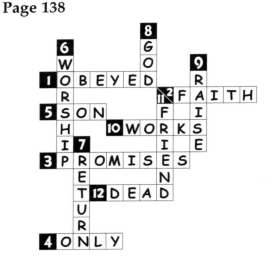

OBSERVATION WORKSHEETS

Chapter 11

1 Now the whole earth used the same language and the same words.

2 It came about as they journeyed east, that they found a plain in the land of Shinar and settled there.

3 They said to one another, "Come, let us make bricks and burn *them* thoroughly." And they used brick for stone, and they used tar for mortar.

4 They said, "Come, let us build for ourselves a city, and a tower whose top *will reach* into heaven, and let us make for ourselves a name, otherwise we will be scattered abroad over the face of the whole earth."

5 The LORD came down to see the city and the tower which the sons of men had built.

6 The LORD said, "Behold, they are one people, and they all have the same language. And this is what they began to do, and now nothing which they purpose to do will be impossible for them.

7 "Come, let Us go down and there confuse their language, so that they will not understand one another's speech."

8 So the LORD scattered them abroad from there over the face of the whole earth; and they stopped building the city.

9 Therefore its name was called Babel, because there the LORD confused the language of the whole earth; and from there the LORD scattered them abroad over the face of the whole earth.

10 These are *the records of* the generations of Shem. Shem was one hundred years old, and became the father of Arpachshad two years after the flood;

11 and Shem lived five hundred years after he became the father of Arpachshad, and he had *other* sons and daughters.

12 Arpachshad lived thirty-five years, and became the father of Shelah;

13 and Arpachshad lived four hundred and three years after he became the father of Shelah, and he had *other* sons and daughters.

14 Shelah lived thirty years, and became the father of Eber;

15 and Shelah lived four hundred and three years after he became the father of Eber, and he had *other* sons and daughters.

16 Eber lived thirty-four years, and became the father of Peleg;

17 and Eber lived four hundred and thirty years after he became the father of Peleg, and he had *other* sons and daughters.

18 Peleg lived thirty years, and became the father of Reu;

19 and Peleg lived two hundred and nine years after he became the father of Reu, and he had *other* sons and daughters.

20 Reu lived thirty-two years, and became the father of Serug;

21 and Reu lived two hundred and seven years after he became the father of Serug, and he had *other* sons and daughters.

22 Serug lived thirty years, and became the father of Nahor;

23 and Serug lived two hundred years after he became the father of Nahor, and he had *other* sons and daughters.

24 Nahor lived twenty-nine years, and became the father of Terah;

25 and Nahor lived one hundred and nineteen years after he became the father of Terah, and he had *other* sons and daughters.

26 Terah lived seventy years, and became the father of Abram, Nahor and Haran.

27 Now these are *the records of* the generations of Terah. Terah became the father of Abram, Nahor and Haran; and Haran became the father of Lot.

28 Haran died in the presence of his father Terah in the land of his
    birth, in Ur of the Chaldeans.

29 Abram and Nahor took wives for themselves. The name of
    Abram's wife was Sarai; and the name of Nahor's wife was
    Milcah, the daughter of Haran, the father of Milcah and Iscah.

30 Sarai was barren; she had no child.

31 Terah took Abram his son, and Lot the son of Haran, his grand-
    son, and Sarai his daughter-in-law, his son Abram's wife; and
    they went out together from Ur of the Chaldeans in order to
    enter the land of Canaan; and they went as far as Haran, and
    settled there.

32 The days of Terah were two hundred and five years; and Terah
    died in Haran.

Chapter 12

1 Now the LORD said to Abram,
   "Go forth from your country,
   And from your relatives
   And from your father's house,
   To the land which I will show you;

2 And I will make you a great nation,
   And I will bless you,
   And make your name great;
   And so you shall be a blessing;

3 And I will bless those who bless you,
   And the one who curses you I will curse.
   And in you all the families of the earth will be blessed."

4 So Abram went forth as the LORD had spoken to him; and Lot
   went with him. Now Abram was seventy-five years old when
   he departed from Haran.

5 Abram took Sarai his wife and Lot his nephew, and all their possessions which they had accumulated, and the persons which they had acquired in Haran, and they set out for the land of Canaan; thus they came to the land of Canaan.

6 Abram passed through the land as far as the site of Shechem, to the oak of Moreh. Now the Canaanite *was* then in the land.

7 The LORD appeared to Abram and said, "To your descendants I will give this land." So he built an altar there to the LORD who had appeared to him.

8 Then he proceeded from there to the mountain on the east of Bethel, and pitched his tent, with Bethel on the west and Ai on the east; and there he built an altar to the LORD and called upon the name of the LORD.

9 Abram journeyed on, continuing toward the Negev.

10 Now there was a famine in the land; so Abram went down to Egypt to sojourn there, for the famine was severe in the land.

11 It came about when he came near to Egypt, that he said to Sarai his wife, "See now, I know that you are a beautiful woman;

12 and when the Egyptians see you, they will say, 'This is his wife'; and they will kill me, but they will let you live.

13 "Please say that you are my sister so that it may go well with me because of you, and that I may live on account of you."

14 It came about when Abram came into Egypt, the Egyptians saw that the woman was very beautiful.

15 Pharaoh's officials saw her and praised her to Pharaoh; and the woman was taken into Pharaoh's house.

16 Therefore he treated Abram well for her sake; and gave him sheep and oxen and donkeys and male and female servants and female donkeys and camels.

17 But the LORD struck Pharaoh and his house with great plagues because of Sarai, Abram's wife.

18 Then Pharaoh called Abram and said, "What is this you have done to me? Why did you not tell me that she was your wife?

19 "Why did you say, 'She is my sister,' so that I took her for my wife? Now then, here is your wife, take her and go."

20 Pharaoh commanded *his* men concerning him; and they escorted him away, with his wife and all that belonged to him.

Chapter 13

1 So Abram went up from Egypt to the Negev, he and his wife and all that belonged to him, and Lot with him.

2 Now Abram was very rich in livestock, in silver and in gold.

3 He went on his journeys from the Negev as far as Bethel, to the place where his tent had been at the beginning, between Bethel and Ai,

4 to the place of the altar which he had made there formerly; and there Abram called on the name of the LORD.

5 Now Lot, who went with Abram, also had flocks and herds and tents.

6 And the land could not sustain them while dwelling together, for their possessions were so great that they were not able to remain together.

7 And there was strife between the herdsmen of Abram's livestock and the herdsmen of Lot's livestock. Now the Canaanite and the Perizzite were dwelling then in the land.

8 So Abram said to Lot, "Please let there be no strife between you and me, nor between my herdsmen and your herdsmen, for we are brothers.

9 "Is not the whole land before you? Please separate from me; if
to the left, then I will go to the right; or if *to* the right, then I will
go to the left."

10 Lot lifted up his eyes and saw all the valley of the Jordan, that it
was well watered everywhere—*this was* before the LORD
destroyed Sodom and Gomorrah—like the garden of the LORD,
like the land of Egypt as you go to Zoar.

11 So Lot chose for himself all the valley of the Jordan, and Lot
journeyed eastward. Thus they separated from each other.

12 Abram settled in the land of Canaan, while Lot settled in the
cities of the valley, and moved his tents as far as Sodom.

13 Now the men of Sodom were wicked exceedingly and sinners
against the LORD.

14 The LORD said to Abram, after Lot had separated from him,
"Now lift up your eyes and look from the place where you are,
northward and southward and eastward and westward;

15 for all the land which you see, I will give it to you and to your
descendants forever.

16 "I will make your descendants as the dust of the earth, so that if
anyone can number the dust of the earth, then your descendants can also be numbered.

17 "Arise, walk about the land through its length and breadth; for I
will give it to you."

18 Then Abram moved his tent and came and dwelt by the oaks of
Mamre, which are in Hebron, and there he built an altar to the
LORD.

Chapter 14

1 And it came about in the days of Amraphel king of Shinar, Arioch
king of Ellasar, Chedorlaomer king of Elam, and Tidal king of Goiim,

2 *that* they made war with Bera king of Sodom, and with Birsha king of Gomorrah, Shinab king of Admah, and Shemeber king of Zeboiim, and the king of Bela (that is, Zoar).

3 All these came as allies to the valley of Siddim (that is, the Salt Sea).

4 Twelve years they had served Chedorlaomer, but the thirteenth year they rebelled.

5 In the fourteenth year Chedorlaomer and the kings that were with him, came and defeated the Rephaim in Ashteroth-kar-naim and the Zuzim in Ham and the Emim in Shaveh-kiriathaim,

6 and the Horites in their Mount Seir, as far as El-paran, which is by the wilderness.

7 Then they turned back and came to En-mishpat (that is, Kadesh), and conquered all the country of the Amalekites, and also the Amorites, who lived in Hazazon-tamar.

8 And the king of Sodom and the king of Gomorrah and the king of Admah and the king of Zeboiim and the king of Bela (that is, Zoar) came out; and they arrayed for battle against them in the valley of Siddim,

9 against Chedorlaomer king of Elam and Tidal king of Goiim and Amraphel king of Shinar and Arioch king of Ellasar—four kings against five.

10 Now the valley of Siddim was full of tar pits; and the kings of Sodom and Gomorrah fled, and they fell into them. But those who survived fled to the hill country.

11 Then they took all the goods of Sodom and Gomorrah and all their food supply, and departed.

12 They also took Lot, Abram's nephew, and his possessions and departed, for he was living in Sodom.

13 Then a fugitive came and told Abram the Hebrew. Now he was living by the oaks of Mamre the Amorite, brother of Eshcol and brother of Aner, and these were allies with Abram.

14 When Abram heard that his relative had been taken captive, he led out his trained men, born in his house, three hundred and eighteen, and went in pursuit as far as Dan.

15 He divided his forces against them by night, he and his servants, and defeated them, and pursued them as far as Hobah, which is north of Damascus.

16 He brought back all the goods, and also brought back his relative Lot with his possessions, and also the women, and the people.

17 Then after his return from the defeat of Chedorlaomer and the kings who were with him, the king of Sodom went out to meet him at the valley of Shaveh (that is, the King's Valley).

18 And Melchizedek king of Salem brought out bread and wine; now he was a priest of God Most High.

19 He blessed him and said,
"Blessed be Abram of God Most High,
Possessor of heaven and earth;

20 And blessed be God Most High,
Who has delivered your enemies into your hand."
He gave him a tenth of all.

21 The king of Sodom said to Abram, "Give the people to me and take the goods for yourself."

22 Abram said to the king of Sodom, "I have sworn to the LORD God Most High, possessor of heaven and earth,

23 that I will not take a thread or a sandal thong or anything that is yours, for fear you would say, 'I have made Abram rich.'

24 "I will take nothing except what the young men have eaten, and the share of the men who went with me, Aner, Eshcol, and Mamre; let them take their share."

Chapter 15

1 After these things the word of the LORD came to Abram in a
vision, saying,

"Do not fear, Abram,

I am a shield to you;

Your reward shall be very great."

2 Abram said, "O Lord GOD, what will You give me, since I am
childless, and the heir of my house is Eliezer of Damascus?"

3 And Abram said, "Since You have given no offspring to me, one
born in my house is my heir."

4 Then behold, the word of the LORD came to him, saying, "This
man will not be your heir; but one who will come forth from
your own body, he shall be your heir."

5 And He took him outside and said, "Now look toward the
heavens, and count the stars, if you are able to count them."
And He said to him, "So shall your descendants be."

6 Then he believed in the LORD; and He reckoned it to him as
righteousness.

7 And He said to him, "I am the LORD who brought you out of Ur
of the Chaldeans, to give you this land to possess it."

8 He said, "O Lord GOD, how may I know that I will possess it?"

9 So He said to him, "Bring Me a three year old heifer, and a three
year old female goat, and a three year old ram, and a turtledove, and a young pigeon."

10 Then he brought all these to Him and cut them in two, and laid
each half opposite the other; but he did not cut the birds.

11 The birds of prey came down upon the carcasses, and Abram
drove them away.

12 Now when the sun was going down, a deep sleep fell upon
Abram; and behold, terror *and* great darkness fell upon him.

13 *God* said to Abram, "Know for certain that your descendants will be strangers in a land that is not theirs, where they will be enslaved and oppressed four hundred years.

14 "But I will also judge the nation whom they will serve, and afterward they will come out with many possessions.

15 "As for you, you shall go to your fathers in peace; you will be buried at a good old age.

16 "Then in the fourth generation they will return here, for the iniquity of the Amorite is not yet complete."

17 It came about when the sun had set, that it was very dark, and behold, *there appeared* a smoking oven and a flaming torch which passed between these pieces.

18 On that day the LORD made a covenant with Abram, saying,
"To your descendants I have given this land,
From the river of Egypt as far as the great river, the river Euphrates:

19 the Kenite and the Kenizzite and the Kadmonite

20 and the Hittite and the Perizzite and the Rephaim

21 and the Amorite and the Canaanite and the Girgashite and the Jebusite."

Chapter 16

1 Now Sarai, Abram's wife had borne him no *children,* and she had an Egyptian maid whose name was Hagar.

2 So Sarai said to Abram, "Now behold, the LORD has prevented me from bearing *children.* Please go in to my maid; perhaps I will obtain children through her." And Abram listened to the voice of Sarai.

3 After Abram had lived ten years in the land of Canaan, Abram's wife Sarai took Hagar the Egyptian, her maid, and gave her to her husband Abram as his wife.

4 He went in to Hagar, and she conceived; and when she saw that she had conceived, her mistress was despised in her sight.

5 And Sarai said to Abram, "May the wrong done me be upon you. I gave my maid into your arms, but when she saw that she had conceived, I was despised in her sight. May the LORD judge between you and me."

6 But Abram said to Sarai, "Behold, your maid is in your power; do to her what is good in your sight." So Sarai treated her harshly, and she fled from her presence.

7 Now the angel of the LORD found her by a spring of water in the wilderness, by the spring on the way to Shur.

8 He said, "Hagar, Sarai's maid, where have you come from and where are you going?" And she said, "I am fleeing from the presence of my mistress Sarai."

9 Then the angel of the LORD said to her, "Return to your mistress, and submit yourself to her authority."

10 Moreover, the angel of the LORD said to her, "I will greatly multiply your descendants so that they will be too many to count."

11 The angel of the LORD said to her further,
"Behold, you are with child,
And you will bear a son;
And you shall call his name Ishmael,
Because the LORD has given heed to your affliction.

12 "He will be a wild donkey of a man,
His hand *will be* against everyone,
And everyone's hand *will be* against him;
And he will live to the east of all his brothers."

13 Then she called the name of the LORD who spoke to her, "You are a God who sees"; for she said, "Have I even remained alive here after seeing Him?"

14 Therefore the well was called Beer-lahai-roi; behold, it is between Kadesh and Bered.

15 So Hagar bore Abram a son; and Abram called the name of his son, whom Hagar bore, Ishmael.

16 Abram was eighty-six years old when Hagar bore Ishmael to him.

Chapter 17

1 Now when Abram was ninety-nine years old, the LORD appeared to Abram and said to him,
"I am God Almighty;
Walk before Me, and be blameless.

2 "I will establish My covenant between Me and you,
And I will multiply you exceedingly."

3 Abram fell on his face, and God talked with him, saying,

4 "As for Me, behold, My covenant is with you,
And you will be the father of a multitude of nations.

5 "No longer shall your name be called Abram,
But your name shall be Abraham;
For I will make you the father of a multitude of nations.

6 "I will make you exceedingly fruitful, and I will make nations of you, and kings will come forth from you.

7 "I will establish My covenant between Me and you and your descendants after you throughout their generations for an everlasting covenant, to be God to you and to your descendants after you.

8 "I will give to you and to your descendants after you, the land of your sojournings, all the land of Canaan, for an everlasting possession; and I will be their God."

9 God said further to Abraham, "Now as for you, you shall keep My covenant, you and your descendants after you throughout their generations.

10 "This is My covenant, which you shall keep, between Me and you and your descendants after you: every male among you shall be circumcised.

11 "And you shall be circumcised in the flesh of your foreskin, and it shall be the sign of the covenant between Me and you.

12 "And every male among you who is eight days old shall be circumcised throughout your generations, a *servant* who is born in the house or who is bought with money from any foreigner, who is not of your descendants.

13 "A *servant* who is born in your house or who is bought with your money shall surely be circumcised; thus shall My covenant be in your flesh for an everlasting covenant.

14 "But an uncircumcised male who is not circumcised in the flesh of his foreskin, that person shall be cut off from his people; he has broken My covenant."

15 Then God said to Abraham, "As for Sarai your wife, you shall not call her name Sarai, but Sarah *shall be* her name.

16 "I will bless her, and indeed I will give you a son by her. Then I will bless her, and she shall be a *mother of* nations; kings of peoples will come from her."

17 Then Abraham fell on his face and laughed, and said in his heart, "Will a child be born to a man one hundred years old? And will Sarah, who is ninety years old, bear *a child?*"

18 And Abraham said to God, "Oh that Ishmael might live before You!"

19 But God said, "No, but Sarah your wife will bear you a son, and you shall call his name Isaac; and I will establish My covenant

with him for an everlasting covenant for his descendants after him.

20 "As for Ishmael, I have heard you; behold, I will bless him, and will make him fruitful and will multiply him exceedingly. He shall become the father of twelve princes, and I will make him a great nation.

21 "But My covenant I will establish with Isaac, whom Sarah will bear to you at this season next year."

22 When He finished talking with him, God went up from Abraham.

23 Then Abraham took Ishmael his son, and all *the servants* who were born in his house and all who were bought with his money, every male among the men of Abraham's household, and circumcised the flesh of their foreskin in the very same day, as God had said to him.

24 Now Abraham was ninety-nine years old when he was circumcised in the flesh of his foreskin.

25 And Ishmael his son was thirteen years old when he was circumcised in the flesh of his foreskin.

26 In the very same day Abraham was circumcised, and Ishmael his son.

27 All the men of his household, who were born in the house or bought with money from a foreigner, were circumcised with him.

Chapter 18

1 Now the LORD appeared to him by the oaks of Mamre, while he was sitting at the tent door in the heat of the day.

2 When he lifted up his eyes and looked, behold, three men were standing opposite him; and when he saw *them,* he ran from the tent door to meet them and bowed himself to the earth,

3 and said, "My lord, if now I have found favor in your sight, please do not pass your servant by.

4 "Please let a little water be brought and wash your feet, and rest yourselves under the tree;

5 and I will bring a piece of bread, that you may refresh yourselves; after that you may go on, since you have visited your servant." And they said, "So do, as you have said."

6 So Abraham hurried into the tent to Sarah, and said, "Quickly, prepare three measures of fine flour, knead *it* and make bread cakes."

7 Abraham also ran to the herd, and took a tender and choice calf and gave *it* to the servant, and he hurried to prepare it.

8 He took curds and milk and the calf which he had prepared, and placed *it* before them; and he was standing by them under the tree as they ate.

9 Then they said to him, "Where is Sarah your wife?" And he said, "There, in the tent."

10 He said, "I will surely return to you at this time next year; and behold, Sarah your wife will have a son." And Sarah was listening at the tent door, which was behind him.

11 Now Abraham and Sarah were old, advanced in age; Sarah was past childbearing.

12 Sarah laughed to herself, saying, "After I have become old, shall I have pleasure, my lord being old also?"

13 And the LORD said to Abraham, "Why did Sarah laugh, saying, 'Shall I indeed bear *a child*, when I am *so* old?'

14 "Is anything too difficult for the LORD? At the appointed time I will return to you, at this time next year, and Sarah will have a son."

15 Sarah denied *it* however, saying, "I did not laugh"; for she was afraid. And He said, "No, but you did laugh."

16 Then the men rose up from there, and looked down toward Sodom; and Abraham was walking with them to send them off.

17 The LORD said, "Shall I hide from Abraham what I am about to do,

18 since Abraham will surely become a great and mighty nation, and in him all the nations of the earth will be blessed?

19 "For I have chosen him, so that he may command his children and his household after him to keep the way of the LORD by doing righteousness and justice, so that the LORD may bring upon Abraham what He has spoken about him."

20 And the LORD said, "The outcry of Sodom and Gomorrah is indeed great, and their sin is exceedingly grave.

21 "I will go down now, and see if they have done entirely according to its outcry, which has come to Me; and if not, I will know."

22 Then the men turned away from there and went toward Sodom, while Abraham was still standing before the LORD.

23 Abraham came near and said, "Will You indeed sweep away the righteous with the wicked?

24 "Suppose there are fifty righteous within the city; will You indeed sweep *it* away and not spare the place for the sake of the fifty righteous who are in it?

25 "Far be it from You to do such a thing, to slay the righteous with the wicked, so that the righteous and the wicked are *treated* alike. Far be it from You! Shall not the Judge of all the earth deal justly?"

26 So the LORD said, "If I find in Sodom fifty righteous within the city, then I will spare the whole place on their account."

27 And Abraham replied, "Now behold, I have ventured to speak
to the Lord, although I am *but* dust and ashes.

28 "Suppose the fifty righteous are lacking five, will You destroy
the whole city because of five?" And He said, "I will not
destroy *it* if I find forty-five there."

29 He spoke to Him yet again and said, "Suppose forty are found
there?" And He said, "I will not do *it* on account of the forty."

30 Then he said, "Oh may the Lord not be angry, and I shall speak;
suppose thirty are found there?" And He said, "I will not do *it*
if I find thirty there."

31 And he said, "Now behold, I have ventured to speak to the
Lord; suppose twenty are found there?" And He said, "I will not
destroy *it* on account of the twenty."

32 Then he said, "Oh may the Lord not be angry, and I shall speak
only this once; suppose ten are found there?" And He said, "I
will not destroy *it* on account of the ten."

33 As soon as He had finished speaking to Abraham the Lord
departed, and Abraham returned to his place.

Chapter 19

1 Now the two angels came to Sodom in the evening as Lot was
sitting in the gate of Sodom. When Lot saw *them*, he rose to
meet them and bowed down *with his* face to the ground.

2 And he said, "Now behold, my lords, please turn aside into
your servant's house, and spend the night, and wash your feet;
then you may rise early and go on your way." They said however,
"No, but we shall spend the night in the square."

3 Yet he urged them strongly, so they turned aside to him and
entered his house; and he prepared a feast for them, and baked
unleavened bread, and they ate.

4 Before they lay down, the men of the city, the men of Sodom, surrounded the house, both young and old, all the people from every quarter;

5 and they called to Lot and said to him, "Where are the men who came to you tonight? Bring them out to us that we may have relations with them."

6 But Lot went out to them at the doorway, and shut the door behind him,

7 and said, "Please, my brothers, do not act wickedly.

8 "Now behold, I have two daughters who have not had relations with man; please let me bring them out to you, and do to them whatever you like; only do nothing to these men, inasmuch as they have come under the shelter of my roof."

9 But they said, "Stand aside." Furthermore, they said, "This one came in as an alien, and already he is acting like a judge; now we will treat you worse than them." So they pressed hard against Lot and came near to break the door.

10 But the men reached out their hands and brought Lot into the house with them, and shut the door.

11 They struck the men who were at the doorway of the house with blindness, both small and great, so that they wearied *themselves trying* to find the doorway.

12 Then the *two* men said to Lot, "Whom else have you here? A son-in-law, and your sons, and your daughters, and whomever you have in the city, bring *them* out of the place;

13 for we are about to destroy this place, because their outcry has become so great before the LORD that the LORD has sent us to destroy it."

14 Lot went out and spoke to his sons-in-law, who were to marry his daughters, and said, "Up, get out of this place, for the LORD

will destroy the city." But he appeared to his sons-in-law to be jesting.

15 When morning dawned, the angels urged Lot, saying, "Up, take your wife and your two daughters who are here, or you will be swept away in the punishment of the city."

16 But he hesitated. So the men seized his hand and the hand of his wife and the hands of his two daughters, for the compassion of the LORD *was* upon him; and they brought him out, and put him outside the city.

17 When they had brought them outside, one said, "Escape for your life! Do not look behind you, and do not stay anywhere in the valley; escape to the mountains, or you will be swept away."

18 But Lot said to them, "Oh no, my lords!

19 "Now behold, your servant has found favor in your sight, and you have magnified your lovingkindness, which you have shown me by saving my life; but I cannot escape to the mountains, for the disaster will overtake me and I will die;

20 now behold, this town is near *enough* to flee to, and it is small. Please, let me escape there (is it not small?) that my life may be saved."

21 He said to him, "Behold, I grant you this request also, not to overthrow the town of which you have spoken.

22 "Hurry, escape there, for I cannot do anything until you arrive there." Therefore the name of the town was called Zoar.

23 The sun had risen over the earth when Lot came to Zoar.

24 Then the LORD rained on Sodom and Gomorrah brimstone and fire from the LORD out of heaven,

25 and He overthrew those cities, and all the valley, and all the inhabitants of the cities, and what grew on the ground.

26 But his wife, from behind him, looked *back,* and she became a pillar of salt.

27 Now Abraham arose early in the morning *and went* to the place where he had stood before the LORD;

28 and he looked down toward Sodom and Gomorrah, and toward all the land of the valley, and he saw, and behold, the smoke of the land ascended like the smoke of a furnace.

29 Thus it came about, when God destroyed the cities of the valley, that God remembered Abraham, and sent Lot out of the midst of the overthrow, when He overthrew the cities in which Lot lived.

30 Lot went up from Zoar, and stayed in the mountains, and his two daughters with him; for he was afraid to stay in Zoar; and he stayed in a cave, he and his two daughters.

31 Then the firstborn said to the younger, "Our father is old, and there is not a man on earth to come in to us after the manner of the earth.

32 "Come, let us make our father drink wine, and let us lie with him that we may preserve our family through our father."

33 So they made their father drink wine that night, and the first-born went in and lay with her father; and he did not know when she lay down or when she arose.

34 On the following day, the firstborn said to the younger, "Behold, I lay last night with my father; let us make him drink wine tonight also; then you go in and lie with him, that we may pre-serve our family through our father."

35 So they made their father drink wine that night also, and the younger arose and lay with him; and he did not know when she lay down or when she arose.

36 Thus both the daughters of Lot were with child by their father.

37 The firstborn bore a son, and called his name Moab; he is the
    father of the Moabites to this day.

38 As for the younger, she also bore a son, and called his name
    Ben-ammi; he is the father of the sons of Ammon to this day.

Chapter 20

1 Now Abraham journeyed from there toward the land of the
   Negev, and settled between Kadesh and Shur; then he
   sojourned in Gerar.

2 Abraham said of Sarah his wife, "She is my sister." So
   Abimelech king of Gerar sent and took Sarah.

3 But God came to Abimelech in a dream of the night, and said to
   him, "Behold, you are a dead man because of the woman whom
   you have taken, for she is married."

4 Now Abimelech had not come near her; and he said, "Lord, will
   You slay a nation, even *though* blameless?

5 "Did he not himself say to me, 'She is my sister'? And she herself said, 'He is my brother.' In the integrity of my heart and the
   innocence of my hands I have done this."

6 Then God said to him in the dream, "Yes, I know that in the
   integrity of your heart you have done this, and I also kept you
   from sinning against Me; therefore I did not let you touch her.

7 "Now therefore, restore the man's wife, for he is a prophet, and
   he will pray for you and you will live. But if you do not restore
   her, know that you shall surely die, you and all who are yours."

8 So Abimelech arose early in the morning and called all his servants and told all these things in their hearing; and the men
   were greatly frightened.

9 Then Abimelech called Abraham and said to him, "What have you done to us? And how have I sinned against you, that you have brought on me and on my kingdom a great sin? You have done to me things that ought not to be done."

10 And Abimelech said to Abraham, "What have you encountered, that you have done this thing?"

11 Abraham said, "Because I thought, surely there is no fear of God in this place, and they will kill me because of my wife.

12 "Besides, she actually is my sister, the daughter of my father, but not the daughter of my mother, and she became my wife;

13 and it came about, when God caused me to wander from my father's house, that I said to her, "This is the kindness which you will show to me: everywhere we go, say of me, "He is my brother.""

14 Abimelech then took sheep and oxen and male and female servants, and gave them to Abraham, and restored his wife Sarah to him.

15 Abimelech said, "Behold, my land is before you; settle wherever you please."

16 To Sarah he said, "Behold, I have given your brother a thousand pieces of silver; behold, it is your vindication before all who are with you, and before all men you are cleared."

17 Abraham prayed to God, and God healed Abimelech and his wife and his maids, so that they bore *children*.

18 For the LORD had closed fast all the wombs of the household of Abimelech because of Sarah, Abraham's wife.

Chapter 21

1 Then the LORD took note of Sarah as He had said, and the LORD did for Sarah as He had promised.

2 So Sarah conceived and bore a son to Abraham in his old age, at the appointed time of which God had spoken to him.

3 Abraham called the name of his son who was born to him, whom Sarah bore to him, Isaac.

4 Then Abraham circumcised his son Isaac when he was eight days old, as God had commanded him.

5 Now Abraham was one hundred years old when his son Isaac was born to him.

6 Sarah said, "God has made laughter for me; everyone who hears will laugh with me."

7 And she said, "Who would have said to Abraham that Sarah would nurse children? Yet I have borne him a son in his old age."

8 The child grew and was weaned, and Abraham made a great feast on the day that Isaac was weaned.

9 Now Sarah saw the son of Hagar the Egyptian, whom she had borne to Abraham, mocking.

10 Therefore she said to Abraham, "Drive out this maid and her son, for the son of this maid shall not be an heir with my son Isaac."

11 The matter distressed Abraham greatly because of his son.

12 But God said to Abraham, "Do not be distressed because of the lad and your maid; whatever Sarah tells you, listen to her, for through Isaac your descendants shall be named.

13 "And of the son of the maid I will make a nation also, because he is your descendant."

14 So Abraham rose early in the morning and took bread and a skin of water and gave *them* to Hagar, putting *them* on her shoulder, and *gave her* the boy, and sent her away. And she departed and wandered about in the wilderness of Beersheba.

15 When the water in the skin was used up, she left the boy under one of the bushes.

16 Then she went and sat down opposite him, about a bowshot away, for she said, "Do not let me see the boy die." And she sat opposite him, and lifted up her voice and wept.

17 God heard the lad crying; and the angel of God called to Hagar from heaven and said to her, "What is the matter with you, Hagar? Do not fear, for God has heard the voice of the lad where he is.

18 "Arise, lift up the lad, and hold him by the hand, for I will make a great nation of him."

19 Then God opened her eyes and she saw a well of water; and she went and filled the skin with water and gave the lad a drink.

20 God was with the lad, and he grew; and he lived in the wilderness and became an archer.

21 He lived in the wilderness of Paran, and his mother took a wife for him from the land of Egypt.

22 Now it came about at that time that Abimelech and Phicol, the commander of his army, spoke to Abraham, saying, "God is with you in all that you do;

23 now therefore, swear to me here by God that you will not deal falsely with me or with my offspring or with my posterity, but according to the kindness that I have shown to you, you shall show to me and to the land in which you have sojourned."

24 Abraham said, "I swear it."

25 But Abraham complained to Abimelech because of the well of water which the servants of Abimelech had seized.

26 And Abimelech said, "I do not know who has done this thing; you did not tell me, nor did I hear of it until today."

27 Abraham took sheep and oxen and gave them to Abimelech, and the two of them made a covenant.

28 Then Abraham set seven ewe lambs of the flock by themselves.

29 Abimelech said to Abraham, "What do these seven ewe lambs mean, which you have set by themselves?"

30 He said, "You shall take these seven ewe lambs from my hand so that it may be a witness to me, that I dug this well."

31 Therefore he called that place Beersheba, because there the two of them took an oath.

32 So they made a covenant at Beersheba; and Abimelech and Phicol, the commander of his army, arose and returned to the land of the Philistines.

33 *Abraham* planted a tamarisk tree at Beersheba, and there he called on the name of the LORD, the Everlasting God.

34 And Abraham sojourned in the land of the Philistines for many days.

Chapter 22

1 Now it came about after these things, that God tested Abraham, and said to him, "Abraham!" And he said, "Here I am."

2 He said, "Take now your son, your only son, whom you love, Isaac, and go to the land of Moriah, and offer him there as a burnt offering on one of the mountains of which I will tell you."

3 So Abraham rose early in the morning and saddled his donkey, and took two of his young men with him and Isaac his son; and he split wood for the burnt offering, and arose and went to the place of which God had told him.

4 On the third day Abraham raised his eyes and saw the place from a distance.

5 Abraham said to his young men, "Stay here with the donkey, and I and the lad will go over there; and we will worship and return to you."

6 Abraham took the wood of the burnt offering and laid it on Isaac his son, and he took in his hand the fire and the knife. So the two of them walked on together.

7 Isaac spoke to Abraham his father and said, "My father!" And he said, "Here I am, my son." And he said, "Behold, the fire and the wood, but where is the lamb for the burnt offering?"

8 Abraham said, "God will provide for Himself the lamb for the burnt offering, my son." So the two of them walked on together.

9 Then they came to the place of which God had told him; and Abraham built the altar there and arranged the wood, and bound his son Isaac and laid him on the altar, on top of the wood.

10 Abraham stretched out his hand and took the knife to slay his son.

11 But the angel of the LORD called to him from heaven and said, "Abraham, Abraham!" And he said, "Here I am."

12 He said, "Do not stretch out your hand against the lad, and do nothing to him; for now I know that you fear God, since you have not withheld your son, your only son, from Me."

13 Then Abraham raised his eyes and looked, and behold, behind *him* a ram caught in the thicket by his horns; and Abraham went and took the ram and offered him up for a burnt offering in the place of his son.

14 Abraham called the name of that place The LORD Will Provide, as it is said to this day, "In the mount of the LORD it will be provided."

15 Then the angel of the LORD called to Abraham a second time from heaven,

16 and said, "By Myself I have sworn, declares the LORD, because you have done this thing and have not withheld your son, your only son,

17 indeed I will greatly bless you, and I will greatly multiply your seed as the stars of the heavens and as the sand which is on the seashore; and your seed shall possess the gate of their enemies.

18 "In your seed all the nations of the earth shall be blessed, because you have obeyed My voice."

19 So Abraham returned to his young men, and they arose and went together to Beersheba; and Abraham lived at Beersheba.

20 Now it came about after these things, that it was told Abraham, saying, "Behold, Milcah also has borne children to your brother Nahor:

21 Uz his firstborn and Buz his brother and Kemuel the father of Aram

22 and Chesed and Hazo and Pildash and Jidlaph and Bethuel."

23 Bethuel became the father of Rebekah; these eight Milcah bore to Nahor, Abraham's brother.

24 His concubine, whose name was Reumah, also bore Tebah and Gaham and Tahash and Maacah.

Chapter 23

1 Now Sarah lived one hundred and twenty-seven years; *these were* the years of the life of Sarah.

2 Sarah died in Kiriath-arba (that is, Hebron) in the land of Canaan; and Abraham went in to mourn for Sarah and to weep for her.

3 Then Abraham rose from before his dead, and spoke to the sons of Heth, saying,

4 "I am a stranger and a sojourner among you; give me a burial site among you that I may bury my dead out of my sight."

5 The sons of Heth answered Abraham, saying to him,

6 "Hear us, my lord, you are a mighty prince among us; bury your dead in the choicest of our graves; none of us will refuse you his grave for burying your dead."

7 So Abraham rose and bowed to the people of the land, the sons of Heth.

8 And he spoke with them, saying, "If it is your wish *for me* to bury my dead out of my sight, hear me, and approach Ephron the son of Zohar for me,

9 that he may give me the cave of Machpelah which he owns, which is at the end of his field; for the full price let him give it to me in your presence for a burial site."

10 Now Ephron was sitting among the sons of Heth; and Ephron the Hittite answered Abraham in the hearing of the sons of Heth; *even* of all who went in at the gate of his city, saying,

11 "No, my lord, hear me; I give you the field, and I give you the cave that is in it. In the presence of the sons of my people I give it to you; bury your dead."

12 And Abraham bowed before the people of the land.

13 He spoke to Ephron in the hearing of the people of the land, saying, "If you will only please listen to me; I will give the price of the field, accept *it* from me that I may bury my dead there."

14 Then Ephron answered Abraham, saying to him,

15 "My lord, listen to me; a piece of land worth four hundred shekels of silver, what is that between me and you? So bury your dead."

16 Abraham listened to Ephron; and Abraham weighed out for Ephron the silver which he had named in the hearing of the sons of Heth, four hundred shekels of silver, commercial standard.

17 So Ephron's field, which was in Machpelah, which faced Mamre, the field and cave which was in it, and all the trees which were in the field, that were within all the confines of its border, were deeded over

18 to Abraham for a possession in the presence of the sons of Heth, before all who went in at the gate of his city.

19 After this, Abraham buried Sarah his wife in the cave of the field at Machpelah facing Mamre (that is, Hebron) in the land of Canaan.

20 So the field and the cave that is in it, were deeded over to Abraham for a burial site by the sons of Heth.

Chapter 24

1 Now Abraham was old, advanced in age; and the LORD had blessed Abraham in every way.

2 Abraham said to his servant, the oldest of his household, who had charge of all that he owned, "Please place your hand under my thigh,

3 and I will make you swear by the LORD, the God of heaven and the God of earth, that you shall not take a wife for my son from the daughters of the Canaanites, among whom I live,

4 but you will go to my country and to my relatives, and take a wife for my son Isaac."

5 The servant said to him, "Suppose the woman is not willing to follow me to this land; should I take your son back to the land from where you came?"

6 Then Abraham said to him, "Beware that you do not take my son back there!

7 "The LORD, the God of heaven, who took me from my father's house and from the land of my birth, and who spoke to me and who swore to me, saying, 'To your descendants I will give this land,' He will send His angel before you, and you will take a wife for my son from there.

8 "But if the woman is not willing to follow you, then you will be free from this my oath; only do not take my son back there."

9 So the servant placed his hand under the thigh of Abraham his master, and swore to him concerning this matter.

10 Then the servant took ten camels from the camels of his master, and set out with a variety of good things of his master's in his hand; and he arose and went to Mesopotamia, to the city of Nahor.

11 He made the camels kneel down outside the city by the well of water at evening time, the time when women go out to draw water.

12 He said, "O LORD, the God of my master Abraham, please grant me success today, and show lovingkindness to my master Abraham.

13 "Behold, I am standing by the spring, and the daughters of the men of the city are coming out to draw water;

14 now may it be that the girl to whom I say, 'Please let down your jar so that I may drink,' and who answers, 'Drink, and I will water your camels also'—*may* she *be the one* whom You have appointed for Your servant Isaac; and by this I will know that You have shown lovingkindness to my master."

15 Before he had finished speaking, behold, Rebekah who was born to Bethuel the son of Milcah, the wife of Abraham's brother Nahor, came out with her jar on her shoulder.

16 The girl was very beautiful, a virgin, and no man had had relations with her; and she went down to the spring and filled her jar and came up.

17 Then the servant ran to meet her, and said, "Please let me drink a little water from your jar."

18 She said, "Drink, my lord"; and she quickly lowered her jar to her hand, and gave him a drink.

19 Now when she had finished giving him a drink, she said, "I will draw also for your camels until they have finished drinking."

20 So she quickly emptied her jar into the trough, and ran back to the well to draw, and she drew for all his camels.

21 Meanwhile, the man was gazing at her in silence, to know whether the Lord had made his journey successful or not.

22 When the camels had finished drinking, the man took a gold ring weighing a half-shekel and two bracelets for her wrists weighing ten shekels in gold,

23 and said, "Whose daughter are you? Please tell me, is there room for us to lodge in your father's house?"

24 She said to him, "I am the daughter of Bethuel, the son of Milcah, whom she bore to Nahor."

25 Again she said to him, "We have plenty of both straw and feed, and room to lodge in."

26 Then the man bowed low and worshiped the Lord.

27 He said, "Blessed be the Lord, the God of my master Abraham, who has not forsaken His lovingkindness and His truth toward my master; as for me, the Lord has guided me in the way to the house of my master's brothers."

28 Then the girl ran and told her mother's household about these things.

29 Now Rebekah had a brother whose name was Laban; and Laban ran outside to the man at the spring.

30 When he saw the ring and the bracelets on his sister's wrists, and when he heard the words of Rebekah his sister, saying, "This is what the man said to me," he went to the man; and behold, he was standing by the camels at the spring.

31 And he said, "Come in, blessed of the LORD! Why do you stand outside since I have prepared the house, and a place for the camels?"

32 So the man entered the house. Then Laban unloaded the camels, and he gave straw and feed to the camels, and water to wash his feet and the feet of the men who were with him.

33 But when *food* was set before him to eat, he said, "I will not eat until I have told my business." And he said, "Speak on."

34 So he said, "I am Abraham's servant.

35 "The LORD has greatly blessed my master, so that he has become rich; and He has given him flocks and herds, and silver and gold, and servants and maids, and camels and donkeys.

36 "Now Sarah my master's wife bore a son to my master in her old age, and he has given him all that he has.

37 "My master made me swear, saying, 'You shall not take a wife for my son from the daughters of the Canaanites, in whose land I live;

38 but you shall go to my father's house and to my relatives, and take a wife for my son.'

39 "I said to my master, 'Suppose the woman does not follow me.'

40 "He said to me, 'The LORD, before whom I have walked, will send His angel with you to make your journey successful, and

you will take a wife for my son from my relatives and from my father's house;

41 then you will be free from my oath, when you come to my relatives; and if they do not give her to you, you will be free from my oath.'

42 "So I came today to the spring, and said, 'O Lord, the God of my master Abraham, if now You will make my journey on which I go successful;

43 behold, I am standing by the spring, and may it be that the maiden who comes out to draw, and to whom I say, "Please let me drink a little water from your jar";

44 and she will say to me, "You drink, and I will draw for your camels also"; let her be the woman whom the Lord has appointed for my master's son.'

45 "Before I had finished speaking in my heart, behold, Rebekah came out with her jar on her shoulder, and went down to the spring and drew, and I said to her, 'Please let me drink.'

46 "She quickly lowered her jar from her *shoulder,* and said, 'Drink, and I will water your camels also'; so I drank, and she watered the camels also.

47 "Then I asked her, and said, 'Whose daughter are you?' And she said, 'The daughter of Bethuel, Nahor's son, whom Milcah bore to him'; and I put the ring on her nose, and the bracelets on her wrists.

48 "And I bowed low and worshiped the Lord, and blessed the Lord, the God of my master Abraham, who had guided me in the right way to take the daughter of my master's kinsman for his son.

49 "So now if you are going to deal kindly and truly with my master, tell me; and if not, let me know, that I may turn to the right hand or the left."

50 Then Laban and Bethuel replied, "The matter comes from the LORD; *so* we cannot speak to you bad or good.

51 "Here is Rebekah before you, take *her* and go, and let her be the wife of your master's son, as the LORD has spoken."

52 When Abraham's servant heard their words, he bowed himself to the ground before the LORD.

53 The servant brought out articles of silver and articles of gold, and garments, and gave them to Rebekah; he also gave precious things to her brother and to her mother.

54 Then he and the men who were with him ate and drank and spent the night. When they arose in the morning, he said, "Send me away to my master."

55 But her brother and her mother said, "Let the girl stay with us *a few* days, say ten; afterward she may go."

56 He said to them, "Do not delay me, since the LORD has prospered my way. Send me away that I may go to my master."

57 And they said, "We will call the girl and consult her wishes."

58 Then they called Rebekah and said to her, "Will you go with this man?" And she said, "I will go."

59 Thus they sent away their sister Rebekah and her nurse with Abraham's servant and his men.

60 They blessed Rebekah and said to her,
"May you, our sister,
Become thousands of ten thousands,
And may your descendants possess
The gate of those who hate them."

61 Then Rebekah arose with her maids, and they mounted the camels and followed the man. So the servant took Rebekah and departed.

62 Now Isaac had come from going to Beer-lahai-roi; for he was living in the Negev.

63 Isaac went out to meditate in the field toward evening; and he lifted up his eyes and looked, and behold, camels were coming.

64 Rebekah lifted up her eyes, and when she saw Isaac she dismounted from the camel.

65 She said to the servant, "Who is that man walking in the field to meet us?" And the servant said, "He is my master." Then she took her veil and covered herself.

66 The servant told Isaac all the things that he had done.

67 Then Isaac brought her into his mother Sarah's tent, and he took Rebekah, and she became his wife, and he loved her; thus Isaac was comforted after his mother's death.

Chapter 25

1 Now Abraham took another wife, whose name was Keturah.

2 She bore to him Zimran and Jokshan and Medan and Midian and Ishbak and Shuah.

3 Jokshan became the father of Sheba and Dedan. And the sons of Dedan were Asshurim and Letushim and Leummim.

4 The sons of Midian *were* Ephah and Epher and Hanoch and Abida and Eldaah. All these *were* the sons of Keturah.

5 Now Abraham gave all that he had to Isaac;

6 but to the sons of his concubines, Abraham gave gifts while he was still living, and sent them away from his son Isaac eastward, to the land of the east.

7 These are all the years of Abraham's life that he lived, one hundred and seventy-five years.

8 Abraham breathed his last and died in a ripe old age, an old man and satisfied *with life;* and he was gathered to his people.

9 Then his sons Isaac and Ishmael buried him in the cave of Machpelah, in the field of Ephron the son of Zohar the Hittite, facing Mamre,

10 the field which Abraham purchased from the sons of Heth; there Abraham was buried with Sarah his wife.

11 It came about after the death of Abraham, that God blessed his son Isaac; and Isaac lived by Beer-lahai-roi.

12 Now these are *the records of* the generations of Ishmael, Abraham's son, whom Hagar the Egyptian, Sarah's maid, bore to Abraham;

13 and these are the names of the sons of Ishmael, by their names, in the order of their birth: Nebaioth, the firstborn of Ishmael, and Kedar and Adbeel and Mibsam

14 and Mishma and Dumah and Massa,

15 Hadad and Tema, Jetur, Naphish and Kedemah.

16 These are the sons of Ishmael and these are their names, by their villages, and by their camps; twelve princes according to their tribes.

17 These are the years of the life of Ishmael, one hundred and thirty-seven years; and he breathed his last and died, and was gathered to his people.

18 They settled from Havilah to Shur which is east of Egypt as one goes toward Assyria; he settled in defiance of all his relatives.

Hebrews 11

1 Now faith is the assurance of *things* hoped for, the conviction of things not seen.

2 For by it the men of old gained approval.

3 By faith we understand that the worlds were prepared by the word of God, so that what is seen was not made out of things which are visible.

4 By faith Abel offered to God a better sacrifice than Cain, through which he obtained the testimony that he was righteous,

God testifying about his gifts, and through faith, though he is dead, he still speaks.

5 By faith Enoch was taken up so that he would not see death; and he was not found because God took him up; for he obtained the witness that before his being taken up he was pleasing to God.

6 And without faith it is impossible to please *Him*, for he who comes to God must believe *that* He is and that He is a rewarder of those who seek Him.

7 By faith Noah, being warned by God about things not yet seen, in reverence prepared an ark for the salvation of his household, by which he condemned the world, and became an heir of the righteousness which is according to faith.

8 By faith Abraham, when he was called, obeyed by going out to a place which he was to receive for an inheritance; and he went out, not knowing where he was going.

9 By faith he lived as an alien in the land of promise, as in a foreign *land*, dwelling in tents with Isaac and Jacob, fellow heirs of the same promise;

10 for he was looking for the city which has foundations, whose architect and builder is God.

11 By faith even Sarah herself received ability to conceive, even beyond the proper time of life, since she considered Him faithful who had promised.

12 Therefore there was born even of one man, and him as good as dead at that, *as many descendants* as the stars of heaven in number, and innumerable as the sand which is by the seashore.

13 All these died in faith, without receiving the promises, but having seen them and having welcomed them from a distance, and having confessed that they were strangers and exiles on the earth.

14 For those who say such things make it clear that they are seeking a country of their own.

15 And indeed if they had been thinking of that *country* from which they went out, they would have had opportunity to return.

16 But as it is, they desire a better *country*, that is, a heavenly one. Therefore God is not ashamed to be called their God; for He has prepared a city for them.

17 By faith Abraham, when he was tested, offered up Isaac, and he who had received the promises was offering up his only begotten *son;*

18 *it was he* to whom it was said, "In Isaac your descendants shall be called."

19 He considered that God is able to raise *people* even from the dead, from which he also received him back as a type.

20 By faith Isaac blessed Jacob and Esau, even regarding things to come.

21 By faith Jacob, as he was dying, blessed each of the sons of Joseph, and worshiped, *leaning* on the top of his staff.

22 By faith Joseph, when he was dying, made mention of the exodus of the sons of Israel, and gave orders concerning his bones.

23 By faith Moses, when he was born, was hidden for three months by his parents, because they saw he was a beautiful child; and they were not afraid of the king's edict.

24 By faith Moses, when he had grown up, refused to be called the son of Pharaoh's daughter,

25 choosing rather to endure ill-treatment with the people of God than to enjoy the passing pleasures of sin,

26 considering the reproach of Christ greater riches than the treasures of Egypt; for he was looking to the reward.

27 By faith he left Egypt, not fearing the wrath of the king; for he endured, as seeing Him who is unseen.

28 By faith he kept the Passover and the sprinkling of the blood, so that he who destroyed the firstborn would not touch them.

29 By faith they passed through the Red Sea as though *they were passing* through dry land; and the Egyptians, when they attempted it, were drowned.

30 By faith the walls of Jericho fell down after they had been encircled for seven days.

31 By faith Rahab the harlot did not perish along with those who were disobedient, after she had welcomed the spies in peace.

32 And what more shall I say? For time will fail me if I tell of Gideon, Barak, Samson, Jephthah, of David and Samuel and the prophets,

33 who by faith conquered kingdoms, performed *acts of* righteousness, obtained promises, shut the mouths of lions,

34 quenched the power of fire, escaped the edge of the sword, from weakness were made strong, became mighty in war, put foreign armies to flight.

35 Women received *back* their dead by resurrection; and others were tortured, not accepting their release, so that they might obtain a better resurrection;

36 and others experienced mockings and scourgings, yes, also chains and imprisonment.

37 They were stoned, they were sawn in two, they were tempted, they were put to death with the sword; they went about in sheepskins, in goatskins, being destitute, afflicted, ill-treated

38 (*men* of whom the world was not worthy), wandering in deserts and mountains and caves and holes in the ground.

39 And all these, having gained approval through their faith, did not receive what was promised,

40 because God had provided something better for us, so that apart from us they would not be made perfect.

Romans 4

1 What then shall we say that Abraham, our forefather according to the flesh, has found?

2 For if Abraham was justified by works, he has something to boast about, but not before God.

3 For what does the Scripture say? "Abraham believed God, and it was credited to him as righteousness."

4 Now to the one who works, his wage is not credited as a favor, but as what is due.

5 But to the one who does not work, but believes in Him who justifies the ungodly, his faith is credited as righteousness,

6 just as David also speaks of the blessing on the man to whom God credits righteousness apart from works:

7 "Blessed are those whose lawless deeds have been forgiven, And whose sins have been covered.

8 "Blessed is the man whose sin the Lord will not take into account."

9 Is this blessing then on the circumcised, or on the uncircumcised also? For we say, "Faith was credited to Abraham as righteousness."

10 How then was it credited? While he was circumcised, or uncircumcised? Not while circumcised, but while uncircumcised;

11 and he received the sign of circumcision, a seal of the righteousness of the faith which he had while uncircumcised, so that he

might be the father of all who believe without being circum-cised, that righteousness might be credited to them,

12 and the father of circumcision to those who not only are of the circumcision, but who also follow in the steps of the faith of our father Abraham which he had while uncircumcised.

13 For the promise to Abraham or to his descendants that he would be heir of the world was not through the Law, but through the righteousness of faith.

14 For if those who are of the Law are heirs, faith is made void and the promise is nullified;

15 for the Law brings about wrath, but where there is no law, there also is no violation.

16 For this reason *it is* by faith, in order that it *may be* in accordance with grace, so that the promise will be guaranteed to all the descendants, not only to those who are of the Law, but also to those who are of the faith of Abraham, who is the father of us all,

17 (as it is written, "A father of many nations have I made you") in the presence of Him whom he believed, even God, who gives life to the dead and calls into being that which does not exist.

18 In hope against hope he believed, so that he might become a father of many nations according to that which had been spo-ken, "So shall your descendants be."

19 Without becoming weak in faith he contemplated his own body, now as good as dead since he was about a hundred years old, and the deadness of Sarah's womb;

20 yet, with respect to the promise of God, he did not waver in unbelief but grew strong in faith, giving glory to God,

21 and being fully assured that what God had promised, He was able also to perform.

22 Therefore it was also credited to him as righteousness.

23 Now not for his sake only was it written that it was credited to him,

24 but for our sake also, to whom it will be credited, as those who believe in Him who raised Jesus our Lord from the dead,

25 He who was delivered over because of our transgressions, and was raised because of our justification.

MORE DISCOVER 4 YOURSELF!™
INDUCTIVE BIBLE STUDIES FOR KIDS

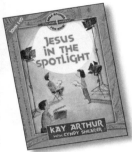

**Kay Arthur
and Cyndy Shearer**
Kids "make" a movie to discover who Jesus is and His impact on their lives. Activities and 15-minute lessons make this study of John 1–10 great for all ages!

ISBN 0-7369-0119-1

Kay Arthur, Janna Arndt, Lisa Guest, and Cyndy Shearer
This book picks up where *Jesus in the Spotlight* leaves off: John 11–16. Kids join a movie team to bring the life of Jesus to the big screen in order to learn key truths about prayer, heaven, and Jesus.

ISBN 0-7369-0144-2

**Kay Arthur
and Janna Arndt**
As "advice columnists," kids delve into the book of James to discover—and learn how to apply—the best answers for a variety of problems.

ISBN 0-7369-0148-5

**Kay Arthur
and Janna Arndt**
This easy-to-use Bible study combines serious commitment to God's Word with illustrations and activities that reinforce biblical truth.

ISBN 0-7369-0362-3

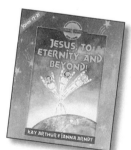

**Kay Arthur and
Janna Arndt**
Focusing on John 17–21, children become "directors" who must discover the details of Jesus' life to make a great movie. They also learn how to get the most out of reading their Bibles.

ISBN 0-7369-0546-4

**Kay Arthur
and Scoti Domeij**
As "reporters," kids investigate Jonah's story and conduct interviews. Using puzzles and activities, these lessons highlight God's loving care and the importance of obedience.

ISBN 0-7369-0203-1

**Kay Arthur
and Janna Arndt**
Kids become archaeologists to uncover how God deals with sin, where different languages and nations came from, and what God's plan is for saving people (Genesis 3–11).

ISBN 0-7369-0374-7

**Kay Arthur
and Janna Arndt**
God's Amazing Creation covers Genesis 1–2—those awesome days when God created the stars, the world, the sea, the animals, and the very first people. Young explorers will go on an archaeological dig to discover truths for themselves!

ISBN 0-7369-0143-4

**Kay Arthur and
Janna Arndt**
The Lord's Prayer is the foundation of this special basic training, and it's not long before the trainees discover the awesome truth that God wants to talk to them as much as they want to talk to Him!

ISBN 0-7369-0666-5

**Kay Arthur and
Janna Arndt**
Readers head out on the rugged Oregon Trail to discover the lessons Abraham learned when he left his home and moved to an unknown land. Kids will face the excitement, fears, and blessings of faith.

ISBN 0-7369-0936-2

Books in the
New Inductive Study Series

∾∾∾∾∾

Teach Me Your Ways
Genesis, Exodus,
Leviticus, Numbers,
Deuteronomy

*Choosing Victory,
Overcoming Defeat*
Joshua, Judges, Ruth

Desiring God's Own Heart
1 & 2 Samuel,
1 Chronicles

Come Walk in My Ways
1 & 2 Kings, 2 Chronicles

*Overcoming Fear and
Discouragement*
Ezra, Nehemiah, Esther

*God's Blueprint for
Bible Prophecy*
Daniel

*Opening the Windows
of Blessing*
Haggai, Zechariah,
Malachi

The Call to Follow Jesus
Luke

*The Holy Spirit
Unleashed in You*
Acts

*God's Answers for
Relationships and Passions*
1 & 2 Corinthians

*Free from Bondage
God's Way*
Galatians, Ephesians

That I May Know Him
Philippians, Colossians

*Standing Firm in
These Last Days*
1 & 2 Thessalonians

*Walking in Power, Love,
and Discipline*
1 & 2 Timothy, Titus

*Living with Discernment
in the End Times*
1 & 2 Peter, Jude

Behold, Jesus Is Coming!
Revelation